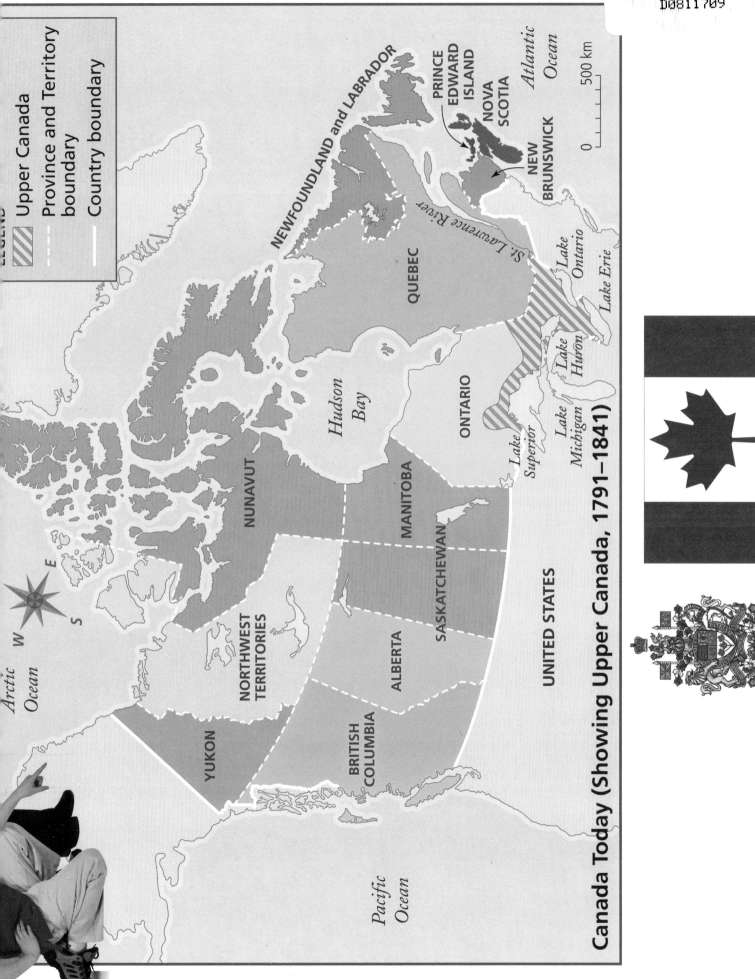

Canada Today (Showing Upper Canada, 1791–1841)

LEGEND

- Upper Canada
- Province and Territory boundary
- Country boundary

Arctic Ocean

Pacific Ocean

Atlantic Ocean

Hudson Bay

YUKON

NORTHWEST TERRITORIES

NUNAVUT

BRITISH COLUMBIA

ALBERTA

SASKATCHEWAN

MANITOBA

ONTARIO

QUEBEC

NEWFOUNDLAND and LABRADOR

PRINCE EDWARD ISLAND

NOVA SCOTIA

NEW BRUNSWICK

UNITED STATES

St. Lawrence River

Lake Superior

Lake Michigan

Lake Huron

Lake Ontario

Lake Erie

500 km

0

Early Settlers

Bruce Henbest

Kim Henbest

Duval House Publishing Inc.

18228 – 102 Avenue
Edmonton, Alberta T5S 1S7
Ph: 1-800-267-6187
Fax: (780) 482-7213
Website: http://www.duvalhouse.com

Authors

Bruce Henbest

Kim Henbest

National Library of Canada Cataloguing in Publication Data

Henbest, Bruce, 1959-

  Early settlers / Bruce Henbest, Kim Henbest.

Includes index.
ISBN 1-55220-220-8

  1. Frontier and pioneer life--Ontario.   I. Henbest, Kim, 1960-   II. Title.

FC3071.H46 2003   971.3'01   C2003-910088-X
F1030.H46 2003

Project Team

Project Manager: Karen Iversen

Editors: Betty Gibbs, Karen Iversen, Shauna Babiuk

Cover and text design: Claudia Pompei (Obsidian Multimedia)

Photo research: David Strand

Production: Claudia Pompei, Leslie Stewart

Maps: Johnson Cartographics Inc., Wendy Johnson

Illustrations: Mitch Fortier, Kim Gluck, Don Hight, Claudia Pompei, Carol Powers

Photographer: Brad Callihoo, New Visions Photography

Photo Shoot Coordinator: Roberta Wildgoose

Cover Illustrations: Mitch Fortier

Manufacturers

Quality Group, Friesens

Photographic Models

Chelsea Cardinal, Ben Lalonde, Shanice Wilson, Randy Wong

Validators

Educational

Pauline Beder, Curriculum Consultant
York Region District School Board

Dolores Cascone, Teacher
Toronto Catholic District School Board

Sandee Elliott, Teacher
Muirhead Elementary School
Toronto, Ontario

Patricia Elliott, B.Ed., M.A., Resource Teacher
Simcoe County District School Board
Midhurst, Ontario

Bias Reviewer

Kennard Ramphal
Scarborough Centre for Alternative Studies
Toronto District School Board
Scarborough, Ontario

Historical

Dr. Jeffrey Keshen
Associate Professor
History Department
University of Ottawa

Peter Cazaly, B.Ed., M.A.
Interpretive Training and Research Officer
Upper Canada Village
Morrisburg, Ontario

Aboriginal Content

Brenda Davis
Educator (Retired)
Six Nations of Grand River

Many website addresses have been identified in this textbook. These are provided as suggestions and are not intended to be a complete resource list. Duval House Publishing does not guarantee that these websites will not change or will continue to exist. Duval House does not endorse the content of the website nor any websites linked to the site. You should consult with your teacher whenever using Internet resources.

We acknowledge the financial support of the Government of Canada through the Book Publishing Industry Development Program (BPIDP) for our publishing activities.

Canadä

Printed and bound in Canada

Acknowledgements

The authors wish to thank all of the people who contributed to the creation of *Early Settlers*. Our involvement would not have happened without the initial vote of confidence from Glenn Rollans. Thanks, Glenn! We are extremely thankful for and wish to acknowledge the guidance, patience, creativity, and hard work of Karen Iversen and Betty Gibbs of Duval House. We also wish to thank all of those involved in the design, production and promotion of the book: designer Claudia Pompei; illustrators Mitch Fortier, Kim Gluck, Don Hight, Claudia Pompei, and Carol Powers; map-maker Wendy Johnson; image seeker David Strand; production artist Leslie Stewart; and all other staff at Duval House who helped to make *Early Settlers* possible. Such a book is truly the work of many hands.

The authors wish to thank family, friends and colleagues within the Upper Canada District School Board, Chesterville Public School, the St. Lawrence Parks Commission, and Upper Canada Village for their support of this project. Lastly, many thanks and much love to our children, Kate and Tom, for their patience, suggestions, and understanding.

Special Thanks to Upper Canada Village

The authors and publisher wish to acknowledge and thank Upper Canada Village for its exceptional contributions to this textbook. Its research library and image collection have been invaluable. Gathering good historical information and images is never an easy task. To preserve the knowledge and re-create images that represent the complexity of our early settlers and their activities takes a tremendous commitment over many years. Without this prior investment, we would simply not have had the resources available to create this textbook for future generations.

Contributors

The authors and publishers wish to thank the following companies and individuals for their contribution to the making of *Early Settlers:*

B & B Publishing
Westmount, Quebec

Bella Music Ltd.
Instruments & Accessories
Edmonton, Alberta

The Flag Shop
Edmonton, Alberta

Knit & Purl
Exquisite Yarn and Knitwears
Edmonton, Alberta

M.E. Wildgoose
Edmonton, Alberta

Photo Credits

Every effort has been made to identify and credit all sources. The publisher would appreciate notification of any omissions or errors so that they may be corrected. All images are copyright © of their respective copyright holders, as listed below. Reproduced with permission.

Legend
(t) = top (r) = right (l) = left (b) = bottom (m) = middle
NAC = National Archives of Canada/Archives nationales du Canada, Ottawa
CMC = Canadian Museum of Civilization
AO = Archives of Ontario

Photos provided by Upper Canada Village: **61** (all); **63** (bl); **69** (all); **70** (all); **72** (all r); **73** (all but tl); **75** (all); **76**; **77** (l); **78** (all r); **81** (all); **82** (all); **83** (all); **84** (all l); **86** (all); **87** (tl) (ml) (bm); **93** (t); **94** (all); **95** (t); **99** (tl) (b); **100** (r); **101** (t); **102** (tl); **103** (br); **104** (all l); **108** (all l); **109** (tl) (br); **110** (all but br); **113** (tr); **117** (tr) (ml) (br); **118** (t) (ml)
front endsheet: source of flag and coat of arms: Department of Canadian Heritage. These images have been reproduced with the permission of the Department of Canadian Heritage, 2003. **5** Wall map reprinted with permission, B&B Wall Maps **8** (tr) Parks Canada (ml, br) Images courtesy of Canadian Tourism Commission **9** (t) Notman & Sandham/NAC/C-005566/acc. #1966-094 **12** (t) Kanata Village, Brantford, Ontario (b) Photograph courtesy of the Royal Ontario Museum © ROM, painting by Ivan Kocsis **13** Permission of Lazare and Parker **14** (br) Crabtree Publishing Company **15** (snowshoes) © CMC, cat. #94-345.1-2, image #S94-8588 **16** (tl) © CMC, from *Canada's Visual History*, Quebec Prehistory, vol. 79, image #21 (mr) © CMC, cat. #BaGg-1:17, image #S96-4622 **20** (tr) Collection of the Woodland Cultural Centre/ photographer: Helena Wilson **27** (br) Photograph courtesy of the Royal Ontario Museum © ROM **29** (br) **30** David Beaucage Johnson **36** (tr) © Canada Post Corporation, 1851. Reproduced with permission **37** (tl) © CMC, from *Canada's Visual History*, Quebec Prehistory, vol. 79, image #30 (b) NAC/C-002774/acc. #1989-401-2 **43** (b) Glanmore National Historic Site of Canada **47** (tr) William Berczy, Thayendanegea (Joseph Brant), National Gallery of Canada, Ottawa (br) Courtesy of the City of Brantford **48** (l) NAC/ C-008111/acc. #1991-30-3 **50** © CMC: (b) cat. #C-12, image #S94-22749; (t) cat. #D-11429, image #S94-24680; (2nd from top) cat. #992.10.118 a-b, image #S94-22452 (detail) **51** (r) Toronto Public Library, from *Canada's Visual History*, British Immigration to British North America, vol. 8 **52** (b) AO, C 233-1-2-2161 **55** (br) Port Credit Harbour, Mississauga, Ontario, Canada; courtesy of the City of Mississauga **56** (tr) Corel Images 462085 (b) The Expositor, Brantford, Ontario **58** Image courtesy of Canadian Tourism Commission (detail) **66** (t) CMC, cat. #A-3159, image #S94-22754 (b) CMC, cat. #D-8831, image #S94-22709 **68** Sharon Rempel, Heritage Wheat Project, Canada (detail) **73** (tl) Photo by Gary Guisinger, courtesy of www.scythesupply.com **74** (t) AO, S-17349 (b) NAC/C-011811/acc. #1983-47-21 **87** (bl) Collection of the Woodland Cultural Centre **90** © Royalty-Free/CORBIS/MAGMA (detail) **91** (tl) NAC, C-024140 **99** (tr) CMC, from *Canada's Visual History*, Upper Canadian furniture, vol. 15, image #2 **106** © Kurt Stier/CORBIS/MAGMA (detail) **109** (tr) National Currency Collection, Currency Museum, Bank of Canada, photography Gord Carter, Ottawa **112** (br) From the Museum of Health Care at Kingston. Used with permission. **113** (l) AO, C 233-1-4-1834 (br) Photograph by Wendy Julien-Crosby **116** © Craig Aurness/CORBIS/ MAGMA **117** (bl) Sharon Rempel, Heritage Wheat Project, Canada **119** (tl) NAC/C-000522 03:04/acc. #1955-128-4 (bl) William Notman & Son/NAC/PA-041333/acc. #1936-271 (br) © Bettmann/CORBIS/MAGMA **120** (tl) The New Brunswick Museum (br) Bob Chambers/Spectrum Stock
back endsheet: Ontario Coat of Arms. Used with permission.

To the Student

Reading and trying the activities in this book are ways to learn about our past. We hope it will be a challenge for you and fun at the same time!

There are many ways to learn about our past. It is a big topic! Often, people start by learning about one part of our past. In *Early Settlers* we look at what was happening in one part of Canada about 200 years ago. You will find pictures, photos, maps, charts, graphs, model-building, stories, and even some drama to help you learn about the past.

Learning about the past is important. It helps us understand why things happened in the past. It also helps us know more about how we live today. We can also compare how we live today with how people lived at another time. Sometimes we discover there have been big changes. Sometimes we find out that many things have stayed the same.

Early Settlers is divided into twelve chapters. These chapters have been put in the order that things happened in the past. As you read, you will find boxes with the name "Legacy." A **legacy** is something of value that has been passed down by people who lived before us. These boxes will tell you about some of the legacies that Aboriginal people and early settlers have passed on to us.

You will also find pictures of activity cards in each chapter. These cards will help you to learn about the jobs people did in the past. We also hope you will make cards like these and use them to play a game. Lastly, you will discover special pages and four Canadian children who invite you to try some fun projects and to learn new skills. We hope you enjoy this book about our past.

Contents

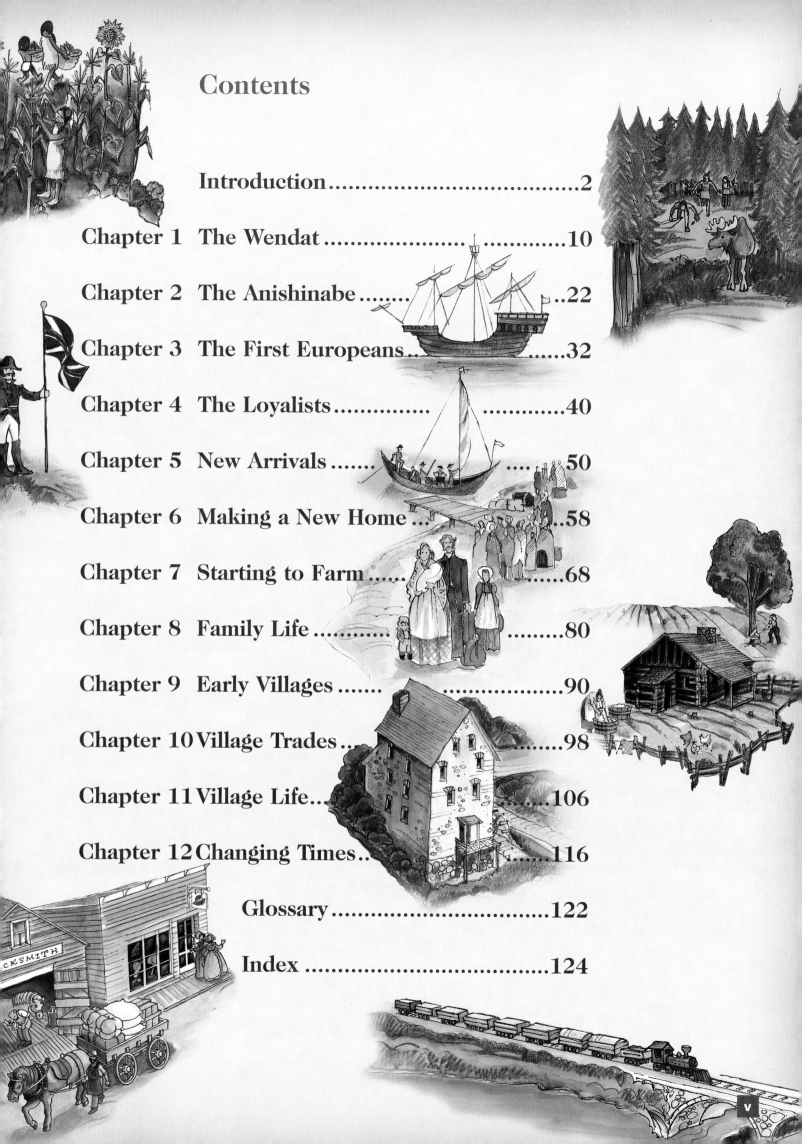

Introduction
Early Settlers

People have not always lived in the place that we call Canada. Different groups of people moved here at different times. Aboriginal people have lived here for many thousands of years. They were the first people. Later, other people moved here. They were called settlers or pioneers. Settlers are people who come to a new place to build homes and communities. The Aboriginal people and settlers helped to make the country that we live in today.

Focus on Learning

In this introduction you will learn about
- map reading
- changes during the time before settlers came to Upper Canada
- the place called Upper Canada

Vocabulary

Aboriginal people	symbols
settlers	climate
history	environment
Upper Canada	Great Lakes
St. Lawrence River	rapids

Do ✛ Discuss ✛ Discover

1. Look carefully at this picture. Is it a picture of life today? What do you think the people are doing? Do you think all these activities happened at the same time? How would you describe this place?

2. As a class, share your ideas about this picture.

3. In your notebook, write two questions about things in this picture that you would like to know more about.

People, Time, and Place

History is about how people lived in the past. This book will show you one part of Canada's history. *Early Settlers* looks at the lives of Aboriginal people and settlers at a particular time in the past. It will show what life was like between 1783 and 1867, more than 130 years ago.

This book also looks at a particular place, Upper Canada. Upper Canada was the name used for part of what we now call Ontario.

Upper Canada

Upper Canada got its name because of the St. Lawrence River. Land further up a river is higher than land closer to the ocean. Upper Canada was further up the St. Lawrence River than Lower Canada. Lower Canada was a part of what we now call the province of Quebec.

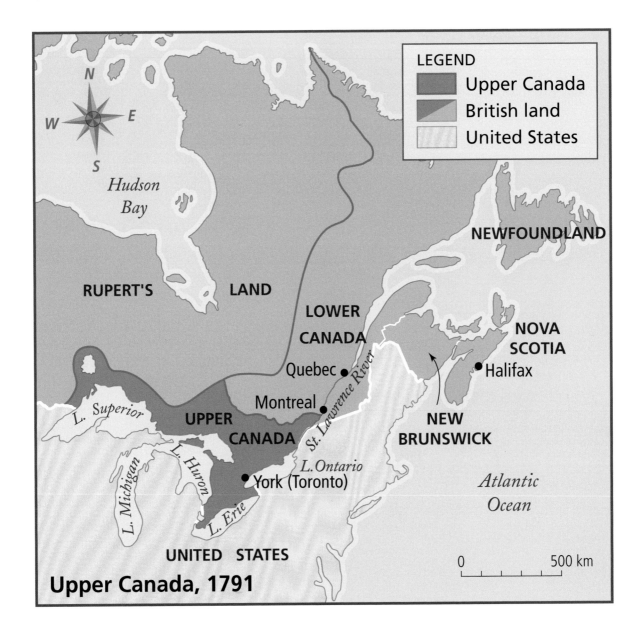

Upper Canada, 1791

Map Reading

Maps are drawings of places as you would see them from above. A map may show a small area, such as a schoolyard, or a large area, such as a country or the world. Maps help us to see where places are. They show how big places are and the distance between places. We can read maps more easily by learning about their parts. The examples below come from the map on page 4.

1. The **title** tells us what the map is about.

2. Maps are drawn carefully. Distances on maps are related to real distances. This is called the **scale**. For example, a map of your schoolyard might have a scale of 1 cm = 1 m. That means that one centimetre on the map is the same as one metre in the schoolyard. Maps of larger areas use a different scale.

3. Map **lines** show many things. For example, lines can be rivers, roads, or borders between areas. Lines are often different colours or widths. This helps you see what they stand for.

4. **Colours** are used to show different areas. For example, water is often shown in blue. Separate countries may be shown by using different colours.

5. **Labels** are the written names on the map. They show important places or areas. Oceans, countries, and larger towns, cities, lakes, and rivers are often labelled.

6. The map **legend** explains what the lines, colours, and other map **symbols** mean. A symbol is a small picture or sign that stands for something. Symbols are used to make maps less crowded and easier to read.

7. A **compass rose** shows which direction on the map is North.

Do ✛ Discuss ✛ Discover

1. Use the map on page 4 to answer these questions:

   a) What parts of the map help you to find Upper Canada?

   b) Is Upper Canada mostly north or south of Lower Canada?

   c) Use the scale to estimate the distance between Montreal and York (Toronto).

5

Think about Time

About 10 000 years ago, the climate of Canada was very cold. Climate means the average weather over a long time. Much of the land was covered with ice.

About 10 000 years ago, the first people were moving across an ice-covered land.

About 5000 years ago, as the climate changed, people's lives started to change.

About 2000 years ago, some Aboriginal people began to grow corn.

These people were the long-ago relatives of the Aboriginal people of today. They worked together to hunt big animals like caribou and woolly mammoths. These people followed the animals that were their food. Their homes also had to move.

Over thousands of years, the climate became warmer and summer lasted longer. Different plants and animals began to live in Upper Canada. The people began to hunt animals like deer, bear, and beaver. They also fished and gathered wild plants to eat.

This was an important change. People growing corn stayed in one place for longer periods of time. They built larger villages.

Corn needs a long, warm summer and good soil to grow. In Upper Canada, only people living in the southern part could grow corn at that time.

The people who lived in the northern part continued to move from place to place and hunt animals for food.

About 500 years ago, people from Europe were exploring and starting to live in parts of Upper Canada.

About 200 years ago, many more people were moving to Upper Canada from the United States and Europe.

Today…

Most of these people did not stay in Upper Canada, but they learned many things from the Aboriginal people. They also changed the Aboriginal people's way of life.

These settlers came for many reasons. They built homes and began villages.

Do ⊕ Discuss ⊕ Discover

Scale is also part of making a timeline.

1. On a page in your notebook, make a line going across that is 10 centimetres long. Put a small line at the beginning and at each centimetre mark, like the example below. Label the first mark "10 000 years ago" and the last mark "Today." Each centimetre equals 1000 years.

2. Above your line, add the times when the other events described on pages 6 and 7 happened.

10 000
years ago

Today

1 cm = 1000 years

Think about Place

The land, water, air, and living things in a place are the **environment**. When settlers came to Upper Canada, they found a forest environment. Many animals and birds made their homes in the forests. There were lots of black flies and mosquitoes in summer.

Upper Canada had a forest environment with many lakes.

Moose were one kind of large animal that lived in the forest.

The Land

In the northern part of Upper Canada, much of the land was rocky. Minerals like copper were found in some areas. The forest included large birch, spruce, and cedar trees.

In the south, most of the land was covered in thick forests. There were huge pine, oak, cedar, elm, and maple trees. The land was less rocky than in the northern part. The soil was better for growing plants.

The Climate

The climate about 200 years ago was similar to today. There were four seasons. Summers were warm and sometimes hot. Winters were cold and there was snow. The ground, lakes, and rivers froze.

The first snow usually fell in late autumn.

Lakes and Rivers

Upper Canada had many lakes, streams, and rivers. Many kinds of plants, fish, and other animals lived in or near these waters.

The largest lakes were Lake Superior, Lake Huron, Lake Erie, and Lake Ontario. These four lakes, along with Lake Michigan, are still called the **Great Lakes**.

The largest and longest river was the St. Lawrence River. It flowed 1197 kilometres from Lake Ontario to the Atlantic Ocean.

Parts of this river were wide and the water flowed slowly. Other places were narrower and the water flowed very quickly over rocks. These places were called **rapids**. Rapids were dangerous for boats travelling on the river.

The Lachine Rapids on the St. Lawrence River were dangerous for travellers.

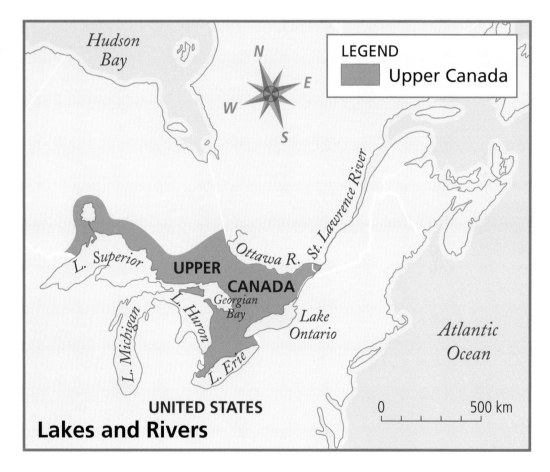

Lakes and Rivers

Do ✛ Discuss ✛ Discover

1. Re-read pages 8 and 9 about the environment of Upper Canada. List one thing that is different today. List three things that are the same today.

2. Study the map on this page. Then, without peeking, find and label the Great Lakes and the St. Lawrence River on a blank copy of this map.

Chapter 1
The Wendat

The Wendat were one of the groups of Aboriginal people living in Upper Canada when people from Europe arrived. The Wendat lived in the southern part of Upper Canada. They grew corn and other crops for food. They lived in large villages. Another name for the Wendat people is the Huron.

Focus on Learning

In this chapter you will learn about
- Aboriginal languages
- where the Wendat lived and what they ate
- the way they travelled and the tools they used
- making graphic organizers
- Wendat families and clans
- Wendat ceremonies and spirits

Vocabulary

Wendat	trading
Anishinabe	awls
longhouses	elders
clearing land	clan
nutrients	ceremonies
preserving	spirits

Aboriginal Languages

Many groups of Aboriginal people lived in Upper Canada long before other people came. These groups lived in different areas. Their ways of life and languages were also different.

Some Aboriginal groups in the southern part of Upper Canada spoke Iroquoian languages. The Wendat were one of these groups. Some other Iroquoian groups moved to Upper Canada later.

Most groups in the northern part of Upper Canada spoke Algonquian languages. The Anishinabe (a/nísh/i/ná/bee) were one of these groups.

Many Aboriginal words are used in English today. For example, the name Canada comes from an Iroquoian word *kanata*. It means "village." The name Ontario is Iroquoian for "beautiful waters." *Moose*, *skunk*, *toboggan*, *Ottawa*, and *tamarack* are all Algonquian words.

Another name for Anishinabe is Ojibwa. You will learn more about the Anishinabe in Chapter 2.

Aboriginal People
Iroquoian languages
Algonquian languages
Wendat (Huron)
Anishinabe (Ojibwa)

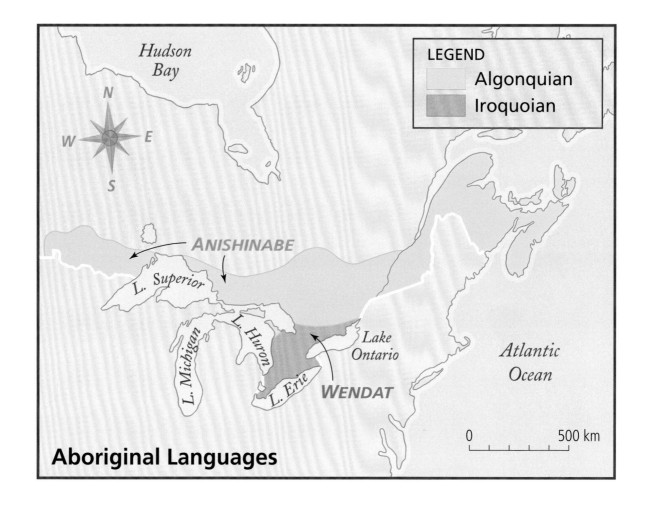

Aboriginal Languages

LEGEND
Algonquian
Iroquoian

Hudson Bay

N
W E
S

ANISHINABE

L. Superior

L. Michigan

L. Huron

L. Erie

WENDAT

Lake Ontario

Atlantic Ocean

0   500 km

Wendat Villages

The Wendat people settled in large villages of up to 1000 or more people. These villages were often built along the shores of rivers. This gave the Wendat a good supply of water. Rivers also made travel easier.

The Wendat built walls around their villages. The walls protected them from attack by enemies. These walls were made out of pointed logs.

Villages were built from materials found in the environment where the Wendat lived.

Wendat villages were protected by high walls.

Homes

Wendat homes were called **longhouses**. These longhouses were between 20 and 40 metres long. They were 7 to 10 metres wide. They had a wooden frame. It was covered with sheets of cedar or elm bark.

Inside, there was one big room with a centre aisle. Several families lived in each longhouse. They slept on wide bunk beds attached to the wall. Top bunks were used to store belongings. Belongings and food were also hung from the frame.

In the centre aisle were fires for cooking and heat. Each fire was shared by two families.

The openings in the longhouse roof let in a little daylight and let out the smoke from the fires.

Food

The Wendat grew a lot of their food. They made fields by **clearing land**. They cut down trees or burned them to make open areas in the forest. Then they planted corn, squash, beans, and sunflowers.

Corn was an important crop. It was dried and ground into small pieces called meal. Cornmeal was used to make flat bread and soup.

The Wendat gathered berries, nuts, edible roots, and plants for food and medicines.

They also hunted deer, elk, moose, bear, rabbits, and beaver. They trapped birds and caught fish for food.

Preserving Food

Preserving food keeps it from spoiling. Corn and beans were dried and stored in bark containers.

Squash and pumpkins were stored in holes dug in the longhouse floor.

Fish and meat were smoked on racks above a fire.

Growing Food

The Wendat cleared land to make fields for their corn and other crops. They loosened the soil with a stick or hoe. Sometimes they put a fish in the bottom of the hole before planting seeds. The fish added **nutrients** to the soil. Nutrients helped to make plants grow healthy and strong.

The Three Sisters

Corn, squash, and beans were called the Three Sisters. The Wendat thought of them as the three daughters of Mother Earth. They were planted together in mounds. The bean vines climbed up the sturdy corn stalks. The squash plants covered the ground around the corn stalks. This kept the ground shaded and moist. These plants also stopped weeds from growing.

Transportation

The Wendat travelled on foot. They made many trails through the woods. There were no roads through the thick forests of Upper Canada at that time. The Wendat did not need them because they had no horses or wagons.

The Wendat also travelled and moved goods by canoe on the lakes and rivers. In winter, the Wendat wore snowshoes to make walking through deep snow easier.

Wendat canoes had a frame made out of wood from an ash tree. This frame was covered with elm bark.

Trading Goods

The Wendat travelled by water to meet other Aboriginal groups. They got goods that they needed by **trading** goods they had grown or made. For example, the Wendat got birchbark canoes from the Anishinabe by trading corn and tobacco. These canoes were lighter and faster than elm bark canoes.

⚥ LEGACY

Snowshoes were invented by Aboriginal people. They are large, so they spread your weight over a larger surface. This stops your feet from sinking into the snow.

Do ✛ Discuss ✛ Discover

1. Look at pages 12 to 15 again. Put the headings Villages, Homes, Food, and Transportation in your notebook. Write two sentences under each heading describing important facts about each topic.

Tools

Spear and arrow points were made from sharpened pieces of bone, stone, or antler.

The Wendat made most of their own tools. They used materials from their environment. This work required skill and a lot of time.

Axes and arrow points were made from stone. The Wendat carefully chipped off small pieces of stone until the tools had sharp edges.

Fish spears and arrow points were sometimes made from deer antlers. Antlers are the hard, solid horns that grow on a male deer's head. Antlers were also used as rakes to loosen the ground before planting seeds.

Knives were made from sharpened stone or bone. Traps, spears, and other weapons were also made from wood, stone, or bone.

Scrapers for scraping corn kernels from the cob were made from a deer's jaw bone. Hoes were made from a deer's hip bone tied to a stick. Smaller bones were sharpened to make **awls**, needles, and fishhooks. An awl is a tool for making holes in leather.

Cooking pots, containers, and pipes for smoking tobacco were made from clay the Wendat dug from the ground.

Wendat clay pots were decorated with patterns of tool marks.

Clues from the Past

Clay cooking pots sometimes cracked when they got too hot. They were thrown out with the burnt food still in them. Scientists have looked at Wendat pots that are hundreds of years old. The pots helped them to discover what the Wendat ate. They found evidence of cornmeal, beans, and fish bones.

Graphic Organizers

One good way to collect and organize information is to create a **graphic organizer**. This is a frame or a picture that you draw to organize information. There are many types of organizers. Charts, diagrams, and webs are three kinds of useful graphic organizers. The example on this page is a chart.

1. Decide what facts you want to show.

2. Choose the type of organizer you think will work.

3. Decide how many parts you will need in your organizer. For example, if you chose to make a chart, how many rows and columns will you need?

4. Add a title.

5. Add headings for each column.

6. Put in your facts where they belong.

Title   Headings

Facts

Wendat Tools			
Tool	**Material**	**Use**	**Picture**
scraper	bone	scrape off corn	
fish spear	antler	catch fish	
cooking pot	clay	cook food	

Family Life

Wendat families worked to meet their needs for food and shelter. Children did not go to school. They learned by watching and copying adults as they worked. They listened to the **elders**. Elders were older people. They were respected and asked about all important decisions.

Men and Boys

The Wendat men and boys cleared land and built longhouses. They made and repaired tools, weapons, and canoes. In the spring, men planted tobacco in small fields. Men and boys hunted and fished to provide some of the family's food.

In summer, many Wendat men made long canoe trips. They traded corn and tobacco with other groups for things the village needed. Men also defended the village when it was attacked.

Women and Girls

Women and girls were responsible for most of the food. In spring, they tapped maple trees to get the sweet sap to drink. They planted corn and other crops. In summer and autumn, they gathered plants from the environment for food and medicine. They also harvested their crops.

Women and girls prepared animal skins to make clothing. They made pots, baskets, trays, and mats out of many materials. Clay, cornhusks, wood strips, grass, and bark were used to make objects for the home.

Grinding corn into meal was hard work.

Women and older girls cared for and taught the children.

Do ⊕ Discuss ⊕ Discover

1. Write down on separate pieces of paper each of the jobs done by Wendat family members; for example, cleared land—men and boys.
2. Take turns drawing a piece of paper and acting out the activity. The rest of the class tries to guess the job and which family members did it.

Making a Clay Pot

You will need:

- clay
- various tools for making marks on your pot

1. Look at the pictures on this page of designs the Wendat used on their clay pots.

2. Collect tools from your environment that you can use to make designs on your clay pot. For example: a pencil, marker top, comb, toothpick, stick.

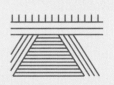

3. Take a small handful of clay and roll it into a ball. Flatten the bottom to make a base.

4. Hollow out the base with your thumbs and fingers.

5. Roll a handful of clay into a long rope.

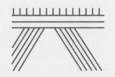

6. Wrap the clay rope around the edge of the base in a coil. Build up the sides of the pot with more lengths of clay rope.

7. Use a flat tool to smooth the sides of the pot.

8. Make designs on your pot using the tools you collected.

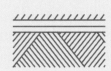

9. Let your pot dry, following the directions on the package of clay.

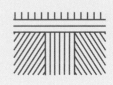

Clans

The Wendat families living in a longhouse belonged to the same **clan**. A clan is a group of families who are related to each other.

Women were the leaders of the clans. When a man married a woman, he went to live with her clan. Children became a part of their mother's clan.

Both men and women were involved in making decisions for the village.

Ceremonies

Wendat **ceremonies** were events that involved a number of special activities. Feasting, music, dancing, special stories, speeches, and tobacco were often part of these ceremonies.

This clay container was used in ceremonies.

Ceremonies were usually held before or after an important task. Gathering maple sap, spring planting, and going on a hunting trip are some examples. A special thanksgiving speech was made in many ceremonies.

Spirits

The Aboriginal people had respect for Mother Earth, who let them use her gifts of plants and animals. They believed in many **spirits**. Spirits are special forces that cannot be seen. Many Aboriginal stories described the powers of these spirits.

Women talked with the clan mother about their concerns.

Using Your Learning

Understanding Concepts

1. Begin an *Early Settlers* New Words section in your notebook. On a blank page, make three columns. Put the headings New Word, Definition, and Sketch at the top of these columns. Pick three words from the vocabulary list at the beginning of this chapter. Write them in the New Word column. Add a definition and make a small sketch for each new word.

Developing Inquiry/Research and Communication Skills

2. Make up a question about the Wendat that you can answer using the information in this chapter. Write your question neatly on one side of an index card. Write the answer on the other side. Give this card to your teacher, who may use it for a game later.

3. Wendat clans had different names. Check the website www.saintemarieamongthe hurons.on.ca/. Click on "Historical Information" and then click on "The Life of the Wendat." Scroll down to "Clans" to find out what the eight clans were called. Record them in your notes.

Applying Concepts and Skills

4. Start a graphic organizer that you can use to compare the Wendat with the Anishinabe. (You will learn about the Anishinabe in the next chapter.)

a) Design your organizer. You will want to look back at some of the headings in this chapter. Remember to give your organizer a title and to put a heading on each part.

Way of Life	Wendat	Anishinabe
Language		
Homes		
Food		

EXAMPLE

b) Meet with a partner to share your ideas. Discuss whether or not your organizers can be improved. Have you forgotten any important topics? Do you have enough room to write?

c) Fill in the information on the Wendat now. (You will add the information on the Anishinabe after you study Chapter 2.)

Chapter 2
The Anishinabe

The Anishinabe spoke an Algonquian language. They lived in the northern part of Upper Canada. Anishinabe families moved often to follow the animals they were hunting. At certain times of the year, many families would come together to work and celebrate.

Focus on Learning

In this chapter you will learn about
- where the Anishinabe lived and what they ate
- the ways they travelled and the tools they used
- their families and clans
- Anishinabe stories and spirits

Vocabulary

wigwams	vision quests
tanning	guardian

Anishinabe Villages

For most of the year, the Anishinabe lived in small camps. Each camp had only a few homes. One family lived in each home.

Animals such as moose moved around. They lived in one area in winter and another in summer. The Anishinabe also moved each season. They needed to be close to the animals they hunted.

Anishinabe families got together in larger groups at certain times of the year. For example, many families worked together to collect maple sap in the spring. They harvested wild rice together in the autumn.

After the work was done, they celebrated and took part in ceremonies. Then, the families moved back to their own hunting places.

Homes

The Anishinabe built homes called wigwams. Many were shaped like domes. Others were like cones. Men and women worked together to build the wigwams.

They used materials from the environment. The frame of the wigwam was made from poles cut from young trees. These poles were bent and tied together. This frame was covered with bark or animal skins.

The Anishinabe put spruce tree branches on the wigwam floor. They covered the branches with animal skins.

A fire was built in the middle of the floor to give heat and to cook food. There was a hole in the top of the wigwam for the smoke to get out.

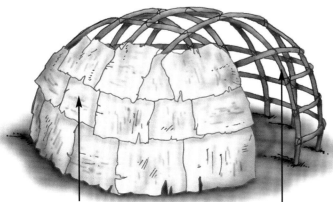

sheets of bark   bent poles

Do ✛ Discuss ✛ Discover

1. Draw your own picture of a wigwam in your notes. Write two sentences below your picture describing how it was built.

Food

The Anishinabe got most of their food by hunting. They also fished and harvested wild rice. They gathered berries, nuts, and wild carrots for food. They collected some plants for medicines. Food was shared among the whole camp.

The land where the Anishinabe lived was rocky. The soil did not have the right nutrients to grow crops well.

Preserving Food

The Anishinabe also preserved and stored food. They dried and smoked meat and fish by hanging it on wooden racks over the fire. They dried and pounded berries into a powder. This food was important during times when there were fewer animals to hunt.

Harvesting Wild Rice

Wild rice is a type of grass that grows in shallow water. The Anishinabe harvested it from a canoe. They always let some seeds fall in the water to grow into plants the next year.

♀ LEGACY

Wild rice is still harvested by Aboriginal people today. It is planted as a crop in places where it did not grow before. You can buy wild rice in a supermarket. The seeds are dark brown.

Hunting Food

The Anishinabe worked hard to get enough food for everyone. They hunted with bows, arrows, and spears. They set snares to catch animals. They hunted moose, caribou, deer, rabbits, beaver, and smaller animals.

Transportation

The Anishinabe travelled and hunted on foot. They carried heavy loads on their backs.

In winter, they wore snowshoes. They pulled their belongings on toboggans.

The Anishinabe also used the water to travel. They made lightweight, fast canoes. These canoes were covered with birchbark. Canoes were often traded to other groups for goods that the Anishinabe needed.

Canoes were an important Aboriginal invention. They made travel much easier and faster. Canoes carried both people and goods. They were used in shallow water and places where other boats could not go. They were not very heavy. This meant they could be carried around rapids and waterfalls.

Europeans who came to North America traded goods to get canoes. They also paid Aboriginal people to help paddle these canoes long distances.

Canoes are still used today to travel and for fun.

Building a Birchbark Canoe

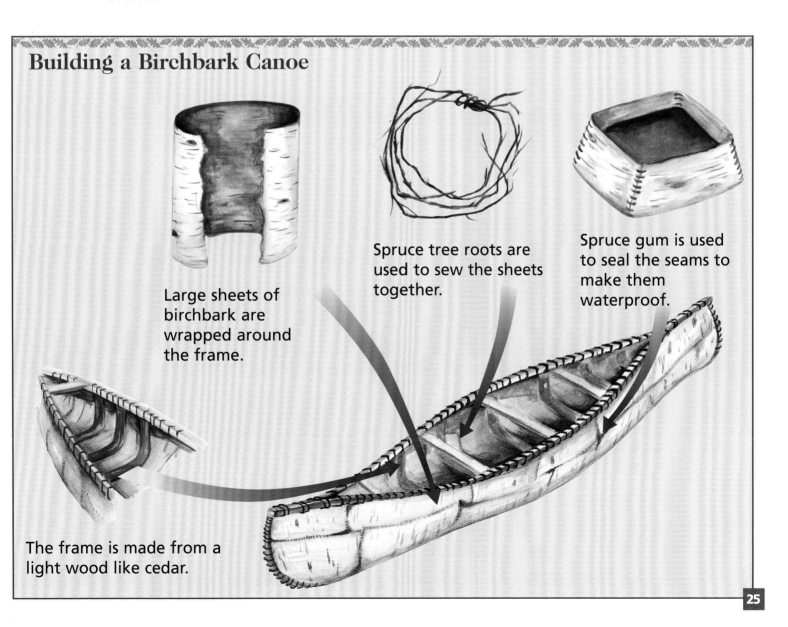

Large sheets of birchbark are wrapped around the frame.

Spruce tree roots are used to sew the sheets together.

Spruce gum is used to seal the seams to make them waterproof.

The frame is made from a light wood like cedar.

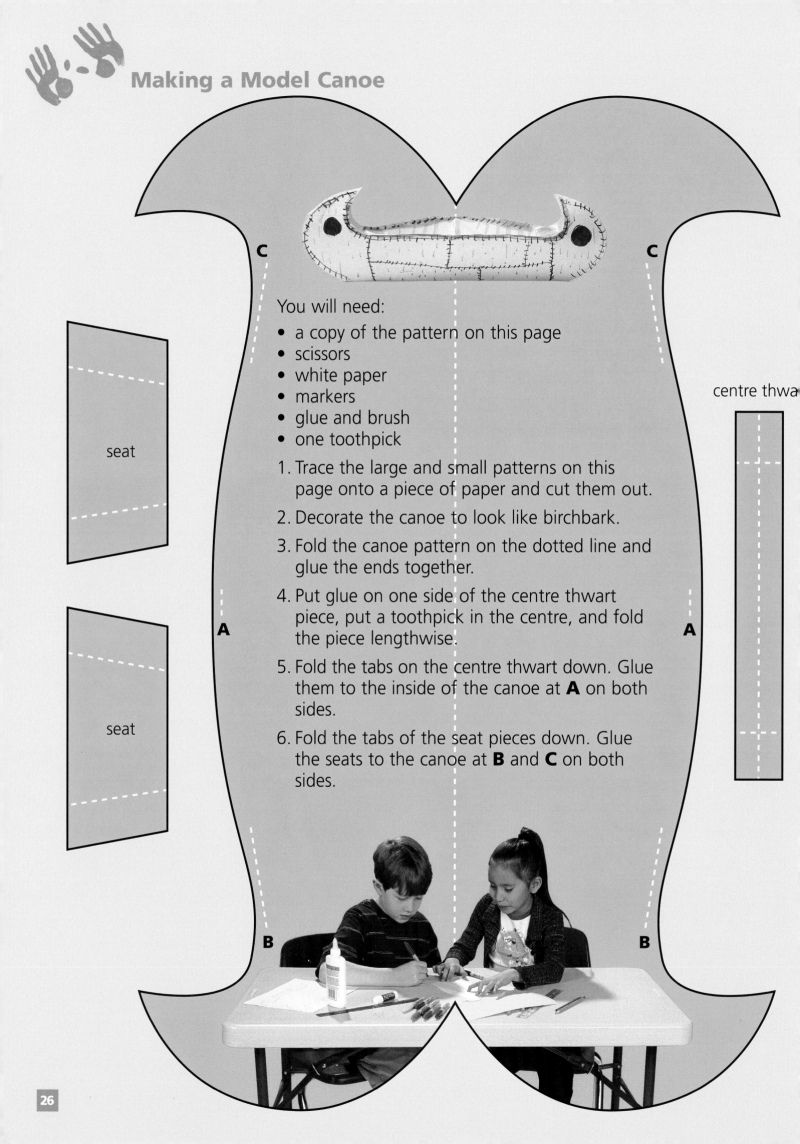

You will need:
- a copy of the pattern on this page
- scissors
- white paper
- markers
- glue and brush
- one toothpick

1. Trace the large and small patterns on this page onto a piece of paper and cut them out.

2. Decorate the canoe to look like birchbark.

3. Fold the canoe pattern on the dotted line and glue the ends together.

4. Put glue on one side of the centre thwart piece, put a toothpick in the centre, and fold the piece lengthwise.

5. Fold the tabs on the centre thwart down. Glue them to the inside of the canoe at **A** on both sides.

6. Fold the tabs of the seat pieces down. Glue the seats to the canoe at **B** and **C** on both sides.

seat

seat

centre thwa

C

C

A

A

B

B

Tools

The Anishinabe used their skills to make tools from many materials in their environment. They used wood, bark, stone, animal skins, bones and antlers. The rope, thread, and glue that held things together were also from the environment.

Knives were made from sharpened bone, antler, or stone.

The Anishinabe used spears, traps, bows, and arrows to hunt. These were made from wood and stone. They fished using bone fishhooks and traps that looked like baskets. The traps were made from woven strips of bark.

Spoons, cups, and pots were made from bark or wood. Bark containers were put together with thin strips of wood, roots, and spruce gum.

A fishing spear had a wooden handle and sharpened bone or antler points.

Large spoons carved from wood were used to scoop up cooked food.

Cooking Without a Metal Pot

How did the Anishinabe cook food using pots made of bark or wood? They put water and meat into the pot. Then, they put stones into the fire to get very hot. They picked up the hot stones with sticks and put them into the pot. The stones heated the water and cooked the meat.

Both Wendat and Anishinabe people collected sap from maple trees to make "sweet water." They used tools and containers like these.

Family Life

Everyone needed to work so the family had enough to eat. Men and older boys hunted and fished. Women and girls gathered berries, nuts, and wild carrots and they cooked food. They prepared animal skins and made clothing.

Men and women worked together for some jobs, like building wigwams. They also made and repaired snowshoes, tools, and other belongings.

Clans

An Anishinabe family was made up of parents, children, grandparents, aunts, uncles, and cousins. These family members belonged to the same clan. Anishinabe children belonged to their father's clan, not their mother's clan. When a girl married, she joined her husband's clan.

Anishinabe children helped in any way they could. They learned by watching and copying adults in their clan. They listened to the elders.

Tanning Leather

The Anishinabe killed animals for food and used their skins for clothing. Some skins were used with the fur left on. Others were tanned. Tanning was a process for making leather. They removed the hair, rubbed other materials into the skin, smoked it over a fire, and softened it.

When it was time to move camp, women and children carried and pulled the belongings. The men hunted animals along the way. They also guarded the family from danger.

Do ⊕ Discuss ⊕ Discover

1. With a partner, discuss how the Anishinabe moved. How was this different from moving today?

Stories and Spirits

Storytelling was an important part of life for Aboriginal people. It was a way they learned about their past. It was a way they shared their beliefs. For example, Aboriginal people showed their respect for Mother Earth in their stories.

Stories were used to teach children important lessons about how to behave.

Spirits

Many Aboriginal stories described the powers of spirits. Their ceremonies showed respect for the spirits and Mother Earth. One spirit of the Anishinabe was Nanabush. Nanabush was a trickster. Sometimes he helped the animals and people. Sometimes he tricked them.

The story on the next page tells how Nanabush helped the turtle get its hard shells.

Vision Quest

Like the Wendat, the Anishinabe believed in **vision quests**. A quest is a journey taken to look for something.

A young man went on a vision quest to meet his **guardian** spirit. A guardian looks after and protects someone else.

The spirit would give the young man a special song. The Wendat and Anishinabe believed that singing this song would make them brave in times of danger.

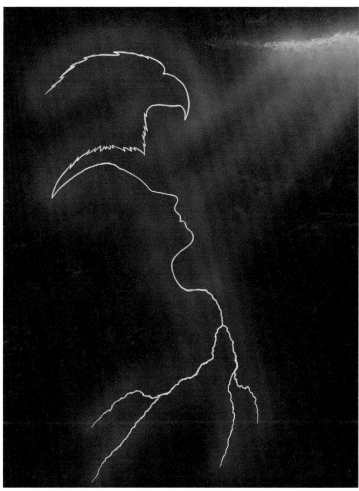

An Anishinabe artist, David Beaucage Johnson, created this painting of a young man's vision. He also painted the picture on the next page.

Nanabush and the Turtle

Long ago, turtles had soft shells. Their shells did not protect them from other animals.

One day, Nanabush was out fishing. He could not seem to catch even the tiniest fish. He wondered where to try his luck next. Nanabush noticed a turtle lying on a rock, sunning itself. He saw an otter creeping toward the turtle. It was getting ready to jump on the turtle.

The turtle heard the otter and ran to hide. He crawled beneath a large piece of bark and pulled in his feet and head. The

otter found no sign of the turtle anywhere. She gave up and went away.

"That was very clever of you, Turtle," said Nanabush. "Now, if you know so much, perhaps you can tell me where the fish are plentiful. I am very hungry."

"Certainly, brother Nanabush," replied the turtle. "Take your spear to that deep pool below the next rapids. You should be able to catch all the fish you need in a few minutes."

Nanabush thanked the turtle. He did what the

turtle said. Nanabush quickly caught enough fish for his dinner.

"Thank you, once again, brother Turtle," he exclaimed. "You have done me a favour! I want to give you a reward. You have little protection against your enemies. Allow me to help you."

Nanabush magically changed the turtle's piece of bark into a hard shell. He placed a second shell underneath the turtle. Just then, he heard another otter coming.

"Ha!" he exclaimed. "We will soon see if these shells protect you. Don't be afraid. I will be nearby in case the otter breaks the shells."

Nanabush hid behind a tree. The otter caught the turtle. However, he could not even dent the shells. Finally, he went away, angry and disgusted.

Nanabush laughed. "There you are, brother Turtle. Your fine house will always protect you from your enemies. Your children and their children's children will also have shells. People will always know that you did a service for Nanabush."

Using Your Learning

Understanding Concepts

1. Pretend you have a birchbark canoe for sale. Write a short newspaper advertisement to sell your canoe. Be sure to include all of its advantages.

2. Add to the *Early Settlers* New Words section in your notebook. Pick one word from the vocabulary list at the beginning of this chapter to add to your section. Write down a definition and make a sketch to help you remember this new word.

Developing Inquiry/Research and Communication Skills

3. Make up a question about the Anishinabe that you can answer using the information in this chapter. Write your question neatly on one side of an index card. Write the answer on the other side. Give this card to your teacher.

4. Go to the Canadian Canoe Museum website: www.canoemuseum.net/ and click on "Our Canoeing Heritage." Find the picture of the birchbark canoe. What colour is it? What colour is the spruce gum? Did you see anything on the website that surprised you?

5. Use the library or Internet to find an Aboriginal story or legend. Read it a few times. Try telling it to your friends without looking at the story. Did the story change when you told it?

Applying Concepts and Skills

6. Finish the graphic organizer comparing the Wendat and Anishinabe that you started on page 21 in the last chapter.

   a) Add information about the Anishinabe under each topic.

   b) Using your organizer, discuss with a partner the ways these groups were the same or different from each other and why.

   c) In your notebook, write one sentence to explain how the Wendat and Anishinabe were the same, and another sentence to explain how they were different.

Chapter 3
The First Europeans

Many of the first Europeans who sailed across the ocean to North America did not come to stay. They came to explore, trade, and take wealth back to their home countries. These Europeans learned many things from the Aboriginal people. During this time, there were many changes to the Aboriginal way of life.

Focus on Learning

In this chapter you will learn about
• European explorers
• how Aboriginal people helped the first Europeans
• the fur trade
• changes to the lives of Aboriginal people
• changes in Upper Canada

Vocabulary

explorers   contagious
fur traders

European Explorers

The first Europeans to come to North America were **explorers**. They came from Britain (England, Scotland, Ireland, Wales), France, Iceland, Netherlands, Portugal, and Spain.

An explorer is someone who comes to find out about a place he or she knows nothing about. Explorers search for new discoveries.

Many of these explorers hoped to find a better way to get to Asia. They did not find one. However, they did find valuable fish and furs. The first explorers who came to Upper Canada were from France. They came in the early 1600s.

The explorers returned to Europe with news of what they had found. There was great interest in getting more furs. More Europeans came to trade with the Aboriginal people for furs.

France claimed the right to trade in certain parts of North America. Upper Canada was one part. France sent soldiers and built forts to protect their fur trade business. In time, these trading posts and forts became villages and towns.

Fort de Lévis was built by French soldiers on an island in the St. Lawrence River. It was near where Prescott is today.

Exploring Places

Explorers crossed the ocean in ships. Then, they travelled up rivers to see what the land was like. Some explorers made maps of the new place. They wrote about their adventures. Some traded goods with the Aboriginal people. They took furs back to their home countries to sell.

Do ✚ Discuss ✚ Discover

1. As a class, discuss reasons why people would explore new places. Make a list on the board and copy it into your notes.

33

Aboriginal Contributions

The first Europeans found life very difficult in North America. It got very cold in winter. The rivers and lakes froze. The deep snow made travel difficult. They had trouble getting or growing enough food to eat. Many became sick and died.

Over time, these explorers, fur traders, and soldiers learned many things from the Aboriginal people. The things they learned helped them to stay alive.

The Cure for Scurvy

Sometimes Europeans travelling to North America got a disease called scurvy. Scurvy is caused by not having enough fresh fruit or vegetables. These types of food were not available during the long trip across the ocean or during the winter. Aboriginal people shared their cure— a tea made from crushed white cedar or spruce needles.

Do ✛ Discuss ✛ Discover

1. Read pages 34–35. Make a web to describe the ways Aboriginal people helped the Europeans. Put the title Aboriginal Contributions in the centre and draw pictures to add to your graphic organizer.

Ways That Aboriginal People Helped the Europeans

❶ **Aboriginal guides** helped the Europeans find their way when they were travelling.

❷ **Aboriginal snowshoes, canoes, and toboggans** helped the Europeans travel and transport loads.

3 Aboriginal knowledge of how to trap and hunt different animals and fish helped the Europeans have enough food.

4 Aboriginal clothing made from animal skins and furs helped the Europeans stay warm in winter.

5 Aboriginal knowledge of plants helped the Europeans treat diseases, grow new crops, and collect foods they needed. For example, maple sap was collected and boiled to make syrup and sugar.

⚲ LEGACY

Maple syrup and sugar are still produced from maple sap today. Many people use maple syrup on pancakes and waffles. Maple is a popular flavour for ice cream and other treats.

The Fur Trade

European **fur traders** traded with Aboriginal people to get beaver furs. They offered goods such as metal knives, copper pots, cloth, glass beads, and guns for these furs. Beaver furs were sent back to Europe by ship. They were sold for high prices.

Felt made from beaver fur was used by European hat makers. These hats were very popular and came in different shapes and styles.

trap beaver

tan hide

transport beaver furs

make hats

 **LEGACY**

The beaver is an important symbol of Canada. A symbol is a picture or sign that stands for something. Pictures of the beaver appear on many items, such as our five cent coin. The beaver was put on Canada's first postage stamp.

Fur Trading

Fur traders paddled their canoes great distances, carrying goods made in Europe. They traded the goods to Aboriginal people in exchange for furs. Fur traders also learned how to use materials from the environment for food and heat. This helped them survive.

Do ⊕ Discuss ⊕ Discover

1. In groups of three, share your ideas about why the beaver became a symbol of Canada.

Ways That the Lives of Aboriginal People Changed

1 Aboriginal people wanted the goods offered by fur traders, such as metal knives, pots, and guns. In time, many Aboriginal people depended on these goods. A number of earlier tools were no longer made or used at all.

2 Europeans sometimes had diseases that were new to Aboriginal people. Several of these diseases were very **contagious**. This means they were easily passed from one person to another. Thousands of Aboriginal people got sick, and many died. Some Aboriginal groups, such as the Wendat, were almost completely destroyed by disease or in battle.

3 Iroquoian and Algonquian groups moved into new areas to get more furs, hunt, and trade.

4 The Anishinabe made more canoes. Special large canoes were built for fur traders so they could carry larger loads.

Changes in Upper Canada

Britain and France were at war in different parts of the world between 1756 and 1763. Some battles were fought in Upper and Lower Canada.

Britain won the war and took control of some of France's land. After the war, French soldiers were allowed to stay. A few settled in Upper Canada.

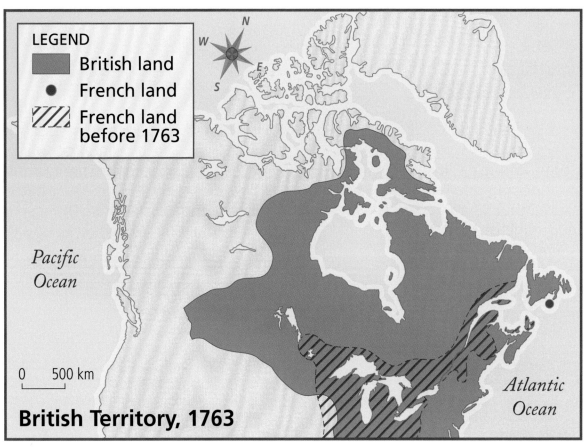

LEGEND
- British land
- French land
- French land before 1763

Pacific Ocean

0   500 km

British Territory, 1763

Atlantic Ocean

By 1763, Britain owned much of France's land in North America, including Upper Canada.

The Union Jack

Britain's flags were flown in Upper Canada. These flags were called jacks. In 1702, the first Union Jack combined the crosses of England and Scotland. In 1801, the cross of Ireland was added. The second Union Jack is still Britain's flag today. Many places, like Canada, once belonged to Britain. Today, the Union Jack is still used on many flags and crests, including Ontario's flag.

A flag is an important symbol.

1702 Union Jack

1801 Union Jack

Ontario flag

Using Your Learning

Understanding Concepts

1. Re-read page 33. Look at the world map inside the front cover of the textbook and find the countries that sent explorers to North America. Label these countries on a blank world map.

2. Look at the painting on page 37. How many people are in the canoe? Why did the fur traders want to use larger canoes? Write your answers in your notebook.

3. a) Pick one word from the vocabulary list and add it to the *Early Settlers* New Words section in your notebook. Write a definition and make a sketch to go with this new word.

   b) Look up a definition for the word "felt." Add this word, the definition, and a sketch to the New Words section in your notebook.

Developing Inquiry/Research and Communication Skills

4. Make up a question about the first Europeans or Aboriginal people that you can answer using the information in this chapter. Write your question neatly on one side of an index card. Write the answer on the other side. Give this card to your teacher.

5. Check out the website www.ainc-inac.gc.ca/ks/ to find out more about Aboriginal contributions to our diet. Click on "Info Sheets" and then "Chances are it's Aboriginal: A Conversation about Aboriginal Foods."

Applying Concepts and Skills

6. There are different Aboriginal legends about how maple syrup was discovered. Do a web search using "maple syrup" + "legend" to find a legend. Read this legend to get some ideas. As a small group, put on a short play to tell the legend to your class.

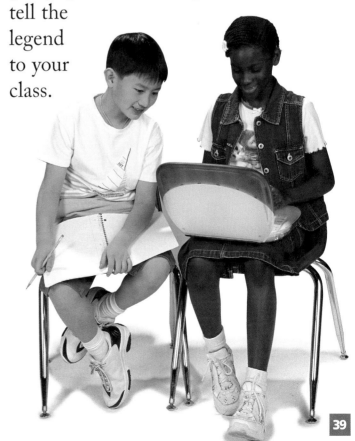

Chapter 4
The Loyalists

Europeans settled in North America in several different colonies. A colony is an area of land governed by another country. Several of the American colonies wanted to join together and become a new country. Some people left these colonies. They were called Loyalists. Many of them came to Upper Canada. The Loyalists were the first large group of settlers to come to Upper Canada.

Focus on Learning

In this chapter you will learn about
- who the Loyalists were
- why they came to Upper Canada
- how land was given to them
- Aboriginal supporters of Britain
- the new leader of Upper Canada
- later American settlers

Vocabulary

colonies	oxen	acres
Loyalists	townships	Six Nations
bateaux	lots	population

The Loyalists

Between 1775 and 1783, Britain and the American colonies were at war. Britain lost the war, and the American colonies formed their own country. This country was the United States of America.

Loyalists were people in the American colonies who supported Britain. The Loyalists moved to other colonies still governed by Britain.

About 100 000 Loyalists left the American colonies. Some were wealthy and some poor. They included many women and children as well as men.

Settlers from European countries who had recently come to the American colonies from places like Germany

Loyalists

Soldiers who fought as part of the British army, along with their families and servants

Aboriginal people who fought on the side of the British

African-American slaves and other African-Americans who fought on the British side

Do ⊕ Discuss ⊕ Discover

1. As a class, discuss what being loyal means.

Why They Left

Loyalists left because they wanted to live in a British colony. They did not want to be part of the new United States.

Loyalists also did not feel safe. Many people were threatened and attacked. Some were put in jail and some were killed. Free African-American Loyalists wanted to keep their freedom.

The British king promised to give the Loyalists food, supplies, and land. This land was in Upper Canada and other British colonies.

Albany, New York   May 1783

My dear sister Mary,

I am writing to tell you that we are leaving the American colonies. In fact, we leave tonight. We supported Britain in this dreadful war. Now that the Americans have won, people who used to be our friends call us awful names. I am so afraid.

Terrible things are happening to Loyalists like us. American soldiers are taking our land. They are putting our men in prisons. Some people have been cruelly hurt with hot tar and feathers. Some have died.

We have to leave our house and most of our belongings. The thought of it makes me cry. We are going to Upper Canada. The King has promised us land, tools, and food if we settle there. The trip will be long and dangerous.

Wish us luck, dear sister, because we shall need it.

Your loving sister, Elizabeth

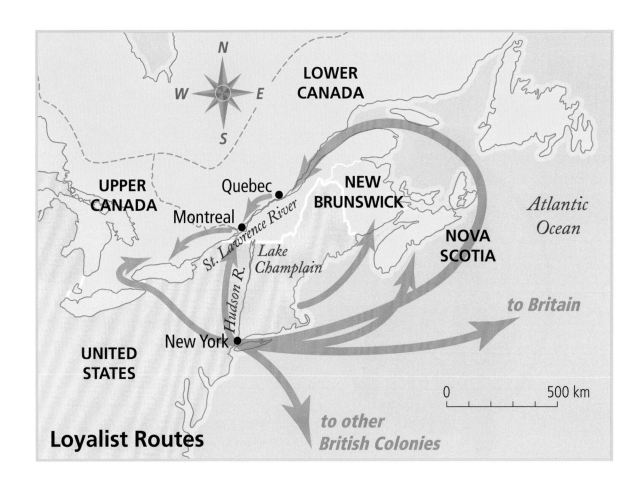

Loyalist Routes

The Long Journey

Many Loyalists went to Nova Scotia by ship. About 10 000 Loyalists headed for Upper Canada. Most of them walked. Some had small horse-drawn wagons. They followed the rivers north towards Montreal. The Loyalists had to leave their homes and many of their belongings behind.

Waiting for Land

The first winter, the Loyalists going to Upper Canada camped near Montreal. It was cold and wet, and many people became ill. They were waiting to find out what land they would get. Finally, land along the St. Lawrence River was chosen.

The Loyalists and their belongings travelled up the river in bateaux to the area where they would settle. Bateaux were flat-bottomed boats, pointed at each end. The bateaux had to get past fast-flowing rapids. Oxen, horses, or men pulled them with ropes. Oxen were large, strong male cattle used for heavy work.

Many Loyalists who travelled to Upper Canada lived in tents along the way.

North to a New Life

"Anna! Are you awake?"

"Yes, John." Anna said softly.

"It's so dark out here," Anna's younger brother said. "I can hardly tell if my eyes are open or shut."

"Are you scared?" Anna asked. She knew he would never admit it. "I'm scared," she said. "It's hard to sleep. I'm cold and I miss my bed. And there are noises in the bushes over there."

"Father would wake up if it was a cougar or a bear," John whispered firmly.

"You're right," she said. "Just wait—tomorrow we'll find it was an old branch making all those sounds."

The next morning, Anna and John packed their blankets in the wagon. Two broken tree branches were swinging and creaking above them.

Samuel Fraser was harnessing the ox. "Hurry, children," he said. "We must move on. It could storm today from the look of that sky. Elizabeth?"

"Coming," his wife replied. In her skirt she carried wild strawberries she had gathered. The fresh fruit would be a treat. The family had been walking along the Hudson River for days.

Soon there will be no food from home left, thought Elizabeth Fraser. She shook her head and reminded herself. That was their old home. They could never go back.

Samuel Fraser led the ox, while Elizabeth walked with Anna and John.

"Will we cross into British lands today, Father?" Anna asked. Samuel could hear the worry and fear in his ten-year-old daughter's voice. He had been a soldier for the British in the war against the American Colonies. When the war was lost, Loyalists like the Frasers had to flee. The Frasers had packed what clothing, tools, food, and furniture would fit on a wagon and left their home in the night.

"Not today, Anna, but soon," said her father. "This river will lead us to Lake Champlain. Once we are past that, we will be safe."

John burst in, "If our farm is close to the water, I want a boat. Will there be neighbours? Might I get a dog? Could I..." His parents and sister laughed.

"One step at a time, young man," his father said.

The wagon wheels creaked, the plodding ox pulled, and the Fraser family walked on. Together, they talked and made plans for their life in a new land.

Getting Land

Land had to be measured and divided before it could be given to the Loyalists. Land near the St. Lawrence River was divided into townships. Each township was divided into smaller pieces of land called lots. Each Loyalist was given one or more lots.

Loyalists received different amounts of land. The amount they got depended on their role in the army and the size of their family. For example, officers got more land than regular soldiers. Some land was also set aside for the Church of England and the government.

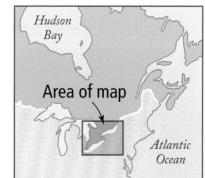

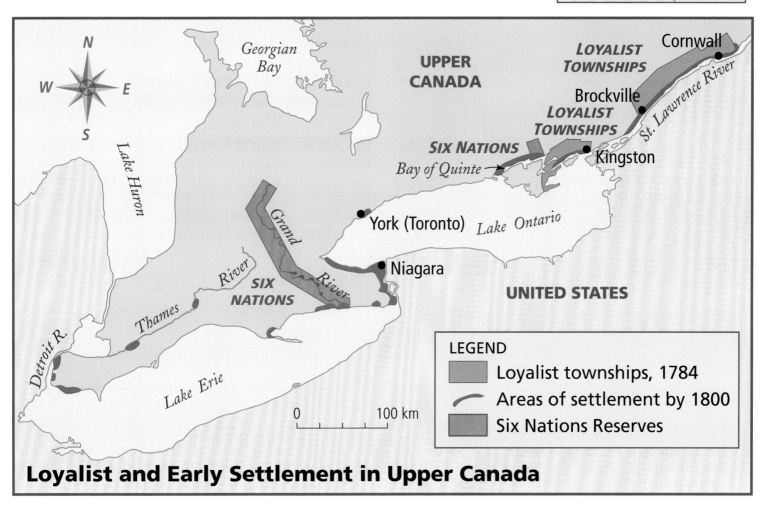

Loyalist and Early Settlement in Upper Canada

This map shows the townships and areas where Loyalists received land and settled.

Do ⊕ Discuss ⊕ Discover

1. On a blank map of Upper Canada, mark the areas where Loyalist townships and Six Nations Reserves were created.

The Luck of the Draw

Many Loyalists had to choose their lot by drawing a ticket from an army officer's hat. They did not know whether their draw was lucky or not. They had to go to their land to find out.

Some lots had good soil. Some had good water nearby. Other lots did not. Loyalists who received more than one lot did not always get lots beside each other. Some Loyalists traded lots with others to get better land.

African-American Loyalists were not treated as equals. Most remained slaves. Free African-Americans did not get land as easily. They did not get as much land, and it was often not good land.

Acres

Lots were measured in **acres**. Acres were a British unit of measurement. One acre is about 0.4 hectares or 4047 square metres. Today, Canadians use metric units of measurement. However, many people still describe farmland using acres.

Amount of Land Received	■ = 50 acres
1000 acres (4 square km) for senior army officers	■■■■■■■■■■■■■■■■■■■■
700 acres (2.8 square km) for army captains	■■■■■■■■■■■■■■
500 acres (2 square km) for junior officers	■■■■■■■■■■
100 acres (0.4 square km) for private soldiers	■■
100 acres (0.4 square km) for a head of the family	■■
50 acres (0.2 square km) for each family member	■

Do ✚ Discuss ✚ Discover

1. Pretend to be a Loyalist. In a sentence or two, describe yourself and your family. Then, show how many acres your family would be given. For example: I am a junior army officer. I am married and I have two children. I would receive 500+50+50+50 = 650 acres.

Aboriginal Supporters

Iroquoian-speaking groups lived south of Lake Ontario when Britain and the American colonies were at war. They were called the **Six Nations**. These nations were the Cayuga, Mohawk, Oneida, Onondaga, Seneca, and Tuscarora.

At first, the Six Nations did not want to support either side. Later, the Cayuga, Mohawk, and most of the Onondaga and Seneca fought for Britain. The Oneida and Tuscarora supported the American colonies. When the war ended, Six Nations people lost their homes and land south of Lake Ontario. Those who supported Britain moved to Upper Canada.

Joseph Brant

Joseph Brant was an important Mohawk leader. He supported the British and convinced many of his people to fight with them.

Joseph Brant wanted his people to be rewarded for their loyalty to Britain. He asked that they be given land in Upper Canada. About 2000 Six Nations people came at the same time as other Loyalists. Many of them settled in the Grand River area. Others settled near the Bay of Quinte. (You can find these places on the map on page 45.)

Thayendanegea (Joseph Brant) by William Berczy, © National Gallery of Canada.

Joseph Brant was also known by his Iroquoian name, Thayendanegea.

⚘ LEGACY

The city of Brantford is named after the famous Mohawk leader, Joseph Brant. His statue stands in a park there.

The New Leader

In 1791, Britain decided that Upper Canada should be a separate province. It should have its own British laws and leaders. The leader of a province was called the Lieutenant Governor.

In 1791, the name Upper Canada was officially chosen.

John Graves Simcoe became the first Lieutenant Governor of Upper Canada. He was a British officer. He fought in the war against the American colonies.

John Simcoe and his wife, Elizabeth, travelled to Upper Canada in 1792. He led the first meetings to pass laws for Upper Canada. Over the next four years, he made many important decisions.

John Simcoe wanted more settlers to come to Upper Canada. He ordered roads to be built. He created more townships and offered land to new settlers.

More American Settlers

American settlers continued to come to Upper Canada for several years. Britain wanted to have people settled on the land. They encouraged Americans to come, and promised them free land. To keep it, the settlers had to clear their land of trees and build a home.

The **population** of Upper Canada grew quickly. The population of a place is all of the people who live there. By 1812, there were four new American settlers for each Loyalist settler in Upper Canada.

After the Loyalists, many more American settlers came to Upper Canada. The population grew rapidly.

Population Graph	⦿ = 10 000 people
1787	⦿
1794	⦿ ⦿
1812	⦿ ⦿ ⦿ ⦿ ⦿ ⦿ ⦿

Using Your Learning

Understanding Concepts

1. On a blank map, label Upper Canada, Lower Canada, New Brunswick, Nova Scotia, and the United States of America. Then add these cities: New York, Quebec, and Montreal. Draw arrows to show the Loyalist routes to Upper Canada.

2. Pick three words from the vocabulary list and add them to the *Early Settlers* New Words section in your notebook. Write a definition and make a sketch to go with each new word.

Developing Inquiry/Research and Communication Skills

3. Make a bar graph showing the same information as the graph on page 48.

4. Make up a question about the Loyalists that you can answer using the information in this chapter. Write your question neatly on one side of an index card. Write the answer on the other side. Give this card to your teacher.

Applying Concepts and Skills

5. Imagine that you and your family had to leave your home quickly. You are moving far away and will not return. You can only take 10 items. With a partner, discuss what items you would take. Make a list of these items. With the class, each pair will discuss one item from their list and why they decided it was important to take.

6. As a class, get a detailed map of your area, divide the map into "lots," and number them. Write the lot numbers on pieces of paper, put them in a hat, and each draw out one. Discuss with a partner whether or not your draw was lucky, and why. Try trading lots with other class members to see if you can get a better lot. Discuss together how this exercise made you feel.

Chapter 5
New Arrivals

By 1812, Britain and the United States were at war again. American settlers were no longer encouraged to come to Upper Canada. Instead, immigrants from Britain were invited. Immigrants are people who move to a new country to live. Many people came to Upper Canada from Britain, so the population continued to grow quickly.

Focus on Learning

In this chapter you will learn about
- who the British immigrants were
- why they came to Upper Canada
- communicating information in a poster
- the journey to Upper Canada
- changes for Aboriginal people

Vocabulary

immigrants	stagecoach
labourers	treaties
tradespeople	Mississauga
typhus	reserves
cholera	

Immigrants from Britain

Between 1812 and 1814, Britain and the United States were at war. They were fighting over control of land. Many battles were fought in Upper Canada.

Britain no longer wanted American settlers to come to Upper Canada. Instead, the British government wanted settlers who would be loyal to Britain.

British soldiers and other immigrants from Britain were encouraged to settle in Upper Canada. They were given land there. In return, they were expected to help protect Upper Canada.

New settlers came to Upper Canada from all over Britain. These immigrants were Scottish, English, Welsh, and Irish. Scotland, England, Wales, and Ireland were all parts of Britain.

A tugboat is pulling this ship out into deeper water. It will sail from England across the Atlantic Ocean.

These new settlers were mostly farmers, labourers, tradespeople, and their families. A labourer is someone who does physical work for someone else. Usually, the work does not need special skills. Tradespeople are workers who have special skills and their own tools.

Immigrants from Britain

(map)

N
W — E
S

SCOTLAND

to Upper Canada

IRELAND

ENGLAND

WALES

to Upper Canada

Atlantic Ocean

0   300 km

Do ✛ Discuss ✛ Discover

1. Look at the world map inside the front cover of this book. Find England, Scotland, Ireland, and Wales. What ocean was crossed to get to Upper Canada?

Why They Left Britain

Settlers came from Britain for different reasons. Many were very poor. They could not find work and had little hope of having a better life where they lived.

In Scotland, many farmers rented land. Their landowners forced them off this land. In Ireland, a disease affected the potato crop. Many people had no food to eat.

Many immigrants came to Upper Canada to find work.

Labourers were needed to build roads and fences, and to work on other projects.

The British offered 100 acres of land to each immigrant family. They gave them money, food, and tools. They paid their transportation from Quebec to their new homes.

At this time, there were very few immigrants to Upper Canada from other parts of the world.

This Scottish farmer and his family are being forced to leave their home, which they rented.

Lands for Sale
IN
Upper Canada.

In 1824, the Canada Company started to advertise land for sale.

Communicating Information in a Poster

A **poster** is a large sign to advertise or give information to people.

In the past, before radio and television, posters were an important way to give information to large numbers of people. Today, posters are still used in many ways.

Keys to making a poster:

1. Decide the purpose of your poster. Who is your audience?

2. Decide what information needs to be included.

3. Decide where the poster will be put up.

4. Make it as big as possible. Keep in mind the space you have.

5. Write the most important words in large letters.

6. Include a picture or photograph.

7. Add colour or a special design to help attract more attention.

Example:

important words

picture

attract attention

Do ⊕ Discuss ⊕ Discover

1. Re-read page 52. In your notebook, list the reasons why British immigrants decided to come to Upper Canada.

2. Add any other possible reasons you have learned about (for example, good water nearby, lots of fish).

3. Use the steps above to make a poster to attract British immigrants to Upper Canada.

Crossing the Ocean

Settlers from Britain crossed the Atlantic Ocean on wooden sailing ships. These ships were crowded, uncomfortable, and dirty. In many cases, there was not enough food or drinking water to last the entire trip. Many people got sick, and many died on these ships.

Diseases like typhus and cholera were common. They spread easily on ships. Typhus is a serious disease passed from person to person by body lice. It causes a high fever, bad headache, and dark red rash. Cholera is caused by bacteria. It is spread in dirty water. Cholera causes vomiting and diarrhea. It was feared because it often caused death.

By this time, the laws about slavery in Upper Canada had changed. More African-Americans escaped slavery and came to Upper Canada.

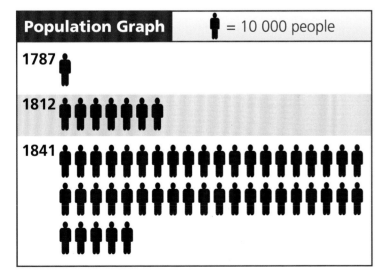

Population Graph	🧍 = 10 000 people
1787	🧍
1812	🧍🧍🧍🧍🧍🧍🧍
1841	🧍🧍

By 1840, the population of Upper Canada grew to more than 400 000 people.

Travel in Canada

1 Ships landed in Quebec.

2 Settlers travelled up the St. Lawrence as far as possible by steamboat.

3 Many of them then continued up the river in bateaux.

4 Some settlers came overland by stagecoach. A stagecoach was a covered vehicle pulled by horses. It was used to carry passengers and the mail.

5 Settlers travelled as far as they could by water or road. Then, they had to walk to their new land.

Do ✚ Discuss ✚ Discover

1. As a class, discuss what the trip across the Atlantic Ocean might have been like for children.

Changes for Aboriginal People

Before the Loyalists came, the British felt that Upper Canada should stay as the hunting lands of the Aboriginal people. Other people were not encouraged to settle there.

By 1783, the British needed land for the Loyalists. They bought land from Aboriginal groups in Upper Canada. These agreements to give up land in exchange for something were called **treaties**.

British officials talked with Aboriginal leaders about treaties to get land for the Loyalists.

The Mississauga Treaties

By this time, the Anishinabe had moved into the southern part of Upper Canada. One group of Anishinabe were the Mississauga people.

Many Six Nations people had lost their homes south of Lake Ontario. The first treaty with the Mississauga was to get land for them.

As more settlers came to Upper Canada, more land was needed. More treaties were signed with the Mississauga.

The British and the Aboriginal people often understood these treaties differently. For example, some Aboriginal people thought they could still hunt on the land. Sometimes the British made promises to get Aboriginal groups to give up their lands. These promises were often broken.

♀ LEGACY

The city of Mississauga gets its name from the Mississauga people who moved into the southern part of Upper Canada in the early 1700s.

Aboriginal Reserves

As new settlers came to Upper Canada, more land was cleared. The large animals of the forest left the areas where there were a lot of settlers. Aboriginal hunting grounds were disappearing.

At first, Aboriginal groups moved to less-settled areas. In time, this was harder to do. By 1830, treaties included making some land into reserves. This meant the Aboriginal groups kept some land as a place to live, hunt, and farm.

During the 1800s, many Anishinabe in southern Upper Canada became farmers.

The first treaties included one payment of money. Under later treaties, groups were paid smaller amounts of money every year. Sometimes the payments were not kept up. This is one reason why today there are many arguments about whether the land was paid for, and who owns it.

Buying Toronto

In 1787, a large piece of land was purchased from the Mississauga. It included the area where Toronto is now. The treaty for this land promised the Mississauga people supplies from Montreal worth 1000 British pounds. Today, that would be about $400 000 worth of supplies.

❦ LEGACY

While there have been many changes, Aboriginal people today still keep parts of their traditional way of life. I.L. Thomas School in Ohsweken is shaped like a turtle. The turtle is an important symbol for the people on the Six Nations reserve.

Using Your Learning

Understanding Concepts

1. Use a map of the world to show where the British immigrants to Upper Canada came from. Be sure to label each part. Look at the map on page 51 for help.

2. Pretend you are a British immigrant. Write a letter to a friend describing your trip from Quebec to your new land in Upper Canada.

3. Pick three words from the vocabulary list and add them to the *Early Settlers* New Words section in your notebook. Write a definition and make a sketch to go with each new word.

Developing Inquiry/Research and Communication Skills

4. Try to think of an English, Scottish, Irish, or Welsh legacy. If you need help, talk to adults about music, food, dancing, clothing, symbols, and holidays. Pick one legacy and learn more about it. Make a short speech to your class about this legacy.

5. Make up a question about British immigrants to Upper Canada that you can answer using the information in this chapter. Write your question neatly on one side of an index card. Write the answer on the other side. Give this card to your teacher.

6. Check the list of treaties on the following website: www.afn.ca/Programs/ Treaties%20and%20Lands% 20Unit/list_of_treaties.htm. Scroll down. When was the first treaty signed in Upper Canada?

Applying Concepts and Skills

7. Compare what you know about the immigrants to Upper Canada with what you know about more recent immigrants to Canada. How are they similar, and how are they different? To start, think about how immigrants came, why, and where they came from. As a class, make a Venn Diagram to compare immigration in the past with immigration today.

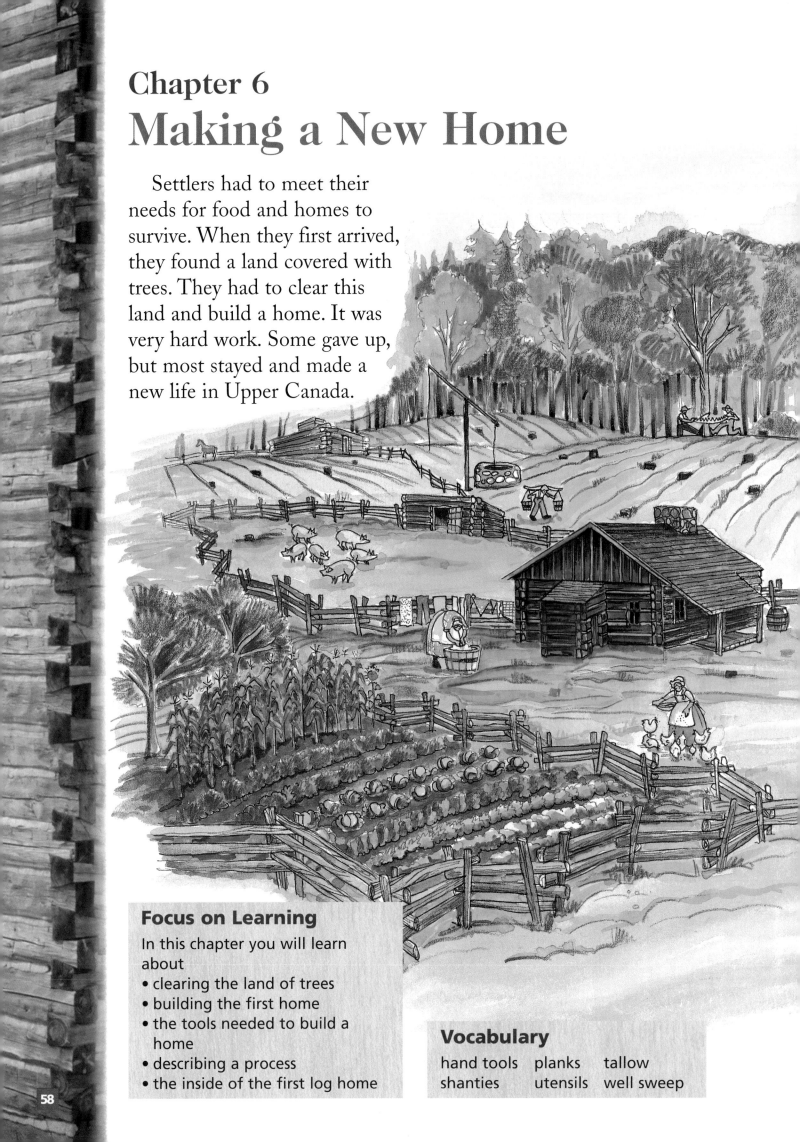

Chapter 6
Making a New Home

Settlers had to meet their needs for food and homes to survive. When they first arrived, they found a land covered with trees. They had to clear this land and build a home. It was very hard work. Some gave up, but most stayed and made a new life in Upper Canada.

Focus on Learning

In this chapter you will learn about
• clearing the land of trees
• building the first home
• the tools needed to build a home
• describing a process
• the inside of the first log home

Vocabulary

hand tools	planks	tallow
shanties	utensils	well sweep

Clearing the Land

Settlers had to cut down large trees to make fields for growing their crops. Most settlers just had a few **hand tools**. Hand tools use only a person's strength to do work. Clearing land with hand tools was very hard work.

Trees were cut down using an axe or large saw. Sometimes they were burned to clear the land. At first, the stumps and roots were left in the field to rot. Then they could be cut or pulled out. Sometimes a team of oxen was used to pull up stumps with chains.

Large logs were kept for building. The smaller branches were burned. Huge numbers of trees were removed to make space for fields, homes, and roads.

Cutting Logs

Settlers used an ox or horse to pull logs to where they would be used. They used different kinds of hand saws to cut wood for building and for firewood. For example, a crosscut saw's metal teeth were made to cut across a piece of wood. Two people pulled the saw back and forth.

LEGACY

Ashes from burned trees were made into potash and sold. Potash was used as a fertilizer. It added potassium to the soil to help plants grow. Potash is still used as a fertilizer today.

Building a Home

The settlers had to build a home right away, before winter came. Their first homes were small, roughly built shelters called **shanties**.

Shanties were made of round logs. They had only one room. There was one door and one or two windows, or none at all. The floor was usually dirt. The chimney was built out of smaller green branches. The cracks between the branches were filled with mud.

Logs were split to cover the roof. The roof was sloped so that rain and snow slid off it.

A Larger Home

After a few years, most settlers built a better home from log, wood, or stone. The logs were often squared instead of left round. Square logs fit together better and joined more tightly at the corners.

The new home had a wooden floor made from thick boards called **planks**. The home was usually larger. It might have more than one room and more windows. There was often an attic above the ceiling. The fireplace was made from stones or brick. There was less danger of fire than from a shanty's wooden chimney.

At first, settlers filled the cracks between the logs with mud mixed with moss or hay to keep out the cold air. Later, they used mortar, a mixture of lime, sand, and water.

Woodcutting Tools

The tools to cut, split, and saw wood were very important. At first, boards were not available. Settlers used round or squared logs to build their homes.

Early settlers used a broad axe to make logs square. A broad axe had a very wide head.

An axe and wooden wedges were used to split smaller logs in half lengthwise. Wedges were pieces of wood shaped like a triangle. They were used for holding or pushing the log apart after the axe had cut into it.

Hand saws, and larger saws called pit-saws, were used to cut planks. Pit-saws had handles at both ends. One person stood on top of the log. The second person stood below in a hole or pit. They pulled the saw blade back and forth.

A hand auger was used to drill holes. Chisels were used to chip out the extra wood between the holes.

These tools made it possible for the settlers to make building material from the trees in their environment. However, the work had to be done by hand. It took time, patience, and strength.

Early settlers did not use nails. Buildings and furniture were put together using wooden pins fitted into holes.

Do ⊕ Discuss ⊕ Discover

1. Choose three of the tools mentioned on this page. Make a graphic organizer to compare these tools with similar tools we use today.

Describing a Process

In a process, something changes into something else. Many processes involve a series of steps for doing something. A graphic organizer called a **flow chart** can help us understand and describe these steps.

1. Decide what process you want to describe. Choose a title.

2. Describe or draw a picture of the material at the beginning of the process.

3. Describe or draw a picture of the final product.

4. Describe or draw the steps that happen in between.

5. Put arrows in your organizer to show how one step follows another.

From Trees to Homes ← title

trees ← material at beginning

logs ← step 1

squared logs   planks and boards ← step 2

log house   wooden furniture ← final product

Inside the Home

Log shanties and homes were plain inside. They had only a few pieces of furniture. Often furniture was used in more than one way. For example, a bench could also be a bed.

Almost all of the furniture and **utensils** were made of wood. Utensils are tools used in the kitchen, such as mixing spoons.

Candle Making

Settlers made candles for light. They cooked animal fat and put the liquid fat into a metal pot. They tied lengths of string to a stick. These were the candle wicks. They dipped the strings down into the pot of liquid fat, and then pulled them up. Then, they let the layer of fat cool. They repeated this until the candle had many layers of tallow around the wick. Thicker candles burned longer.

Heat and Light

The fireplace provided heat for comfort and cooking. It also gave some light. Settlers burned wood in their fireplace.

Settlers relied on light from the sun to do their work. They also burned **tallow** candles and used lamps that burned tallow. Tallow is made from animal fat. Later, coal oil was used. Coal oil is also called kerosene. It is made from oil found under the ground.

Do ✛ Discuss ✛ Discover

1. Make a flow chart to show the steps that settlers followed to make tallow candles. Look back at page 62 for help.

Beds

Settlers slept on wood-framed beds. The mattress was often supported by ropes or wooden boards. Mattresses were like a large cloth pillowcase stuffed with something soft, such as leaves or straw.

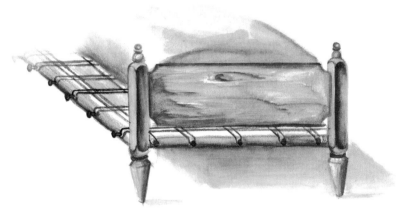

Beds were often attached to the wall to save space. If the home had an attic, it was used for sleeping.

Sleep Tight

Has anyone ever told you to "sleep tight" when you were going to bed? The early settlers were more likely to have a good night's sleep if the ropes under their mattresses were tight.

Do ✛ Discuss ✛ Discover

1. Write a short paragraph in your notebook about the ways early settlers got water to use every day.

Water

It was important to have good drinking water. Settlers carried water in wooden buckets. Sometimes they used a wooden yoke over their shoulders to carry heavy loads.

Some settlers were lucky to live near a small stream or river. Most had to dig a well in the ground to get drinking water.

Wells often had stone walls to hold back the dirt. This kept the water clean. Water was raised up the well using a bucket on a rope. One way of lowering the water bucket and raising water from the well was to use a well sweep.

A weight on the end of the well sweep made lifting the water easier.

Making a Well Sweep

You will need:

- one tree branch about 40 to 60 cm long
- one smaller branch with a "Y"
- plasticine
- string and paper clip
- small paper cup with a flat bottom
- cardboard base 10 cm by 30 cm

1. Make a small hill out of plasticine. Attach it to the cardboard base.

2. Push the bottom end of the Y-shaped branch into the plasticine so the branch stands up.

3. Make a well out of cardboard or plasticine. Attach it near one end of the cardboard base.

4. Tie a short piece of string to one end of the longer branch. Tie the other end of the string to the paper clip. Open the paper clip a little to make a hook.

5. Attach a string or strip of paper across the top of your paper cup to make a handle.

6. Place the long branch on the "Y." Now you have a sweep. Use it to lower the bucket into the well.

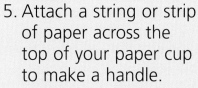

Personal Belongings

Settlers had few personal belongings. Most had only a few clothes and one pair of shoes. Children often went without shoes, especially in summer.

This portable desk was used to hold letters and important papers.

Shirts, pants, and underclothes were often sewn at home from cotton or wool cloth. Socks were knitted by hand. Shoes were made from leather. Sometimes they were made and repaired at home.

Privacy

Early settlers had little privacy in their homes. Often family members shared a bed. There were few rooms and often only one or two sources of light.

Toilets

Settlers did not have toilets inside their homes. Instead, each family built a small wooden building nearby called an outhouse. It had wooden seats. There was a large hole dug beneath it. Another name for an outhouse was a privy.

Wooden chests like this held clothing, bedding, or personal belongings.

Using Your Learning

Understanding Concepts

1. What materials from their environment did settlers use to make and furnish their homes? List these materials and some examples of products in your notebook.

2. Sketch a picture to show the ways that settlers got light into their home.

3. a) Pick three words from the vocabulary list and add them to the *Early Settlers* New Words section in your notebook. Write a definition and make a sketch to go with each new word.

   b) Look up the word "privy" in the dictionary. Add this word, a definition, and a sketch to your New Words section.

Developing Inquiry/Research and Communication Skills

4. Make up a question about settlers' homes that you can answer using information in this chapter. Write your question neatly on one side of an index card. Write the answer on the other side. Give this card to your teacher.

5. Research what candles are made of today. Are they made for the same reasons as in the past? Write your answers in your notebook.

6. Re-read pages 63 and 64. Create a diorama that shows the inside of a shanty or log house.

Applying Concepts and Skills

7. Over the years, settlers built bigger and better homes for themselves. Draw and label pictures of a shanty, a log house, and a house today. Make sure to show how these houses have changed.

8. Think about the things in your home. With a partner, identify two things that are similar to those of the settlers, and two things that are different.

Chapter 7
Starting to Farm

Early settlers had to farm in order to survive. They grew crops and vegetables and raised animals. Besides a home, they needed other buildings, fences, and vehicles. Travel by road was difficult. Settlers grew and stored most of their own food.

Focus on Learning

In this chapter you will learn about
- farming and raising animals
- farm buildings and fences
- farming tools and equipment
- transportation in Upper Canada
- growing and preserving food

Vocabulary

livestock	team
manure	corduroy roads
harvest	canals
threshing	root cellar

Farming

In the first few years, settlers worked hard to clear a few acres of land. Crops were planted as soon as possible.

Settlers grew wheat, corn, other grains, and vegetables to eat. They grew hay and vegetables to feed animals.

Apple, plum, and other trees were planted to supply fruit.

Flax was grown for the fibres in the plant stem. These fibres were made into linen thread. The thread was woven into cloth for clothing.

Raising Animals

Farm animals were called livestock. They were important on the farm. Horses and oxen pulled plows and wagons.

Pigs and most other animals were raised for meat.

Cows provided milk and sheep provided wool. Chickens, ducks, and geese gave eggs and feathers.

Do ✛ Discuss ✛ Discover

1. As a class, discuss how settlers got their food. How do we get our food today? Would you make a good settler? Why or why not?

Farm Buildings

At first, settlers had to let their cows and other animals search for food in the forest. As soon as they could, settlers built sheds and barns. These buildings protected livestock from wild animals and the cold.

Barns were also used for storing hay to feed animals during the winter.

Smokehouses were built to preserve meat. Smoked meat did not spoil as quickly as fresh meat.

Barns and other buildings were usually made from logs. Woodsheds kept wood dry so it would burn better. Drivesheds protected wagons and other farm equipment.

Building Fences

Settlers were expected to build fences to keep their animals from wandering.

The first fences were made from logs. Later, cedar rail fences were built. To make rails, cedar trees were split with an axe and wedges. Wooden board fences were built when boards became more available.

Snake rail fences were one of the earliest kinds of rail fences built.

Settlers built fences to protect crops, fruit trees, and gardens from being eaten by animals.

Making a Snake Rail Fence

You will need:

- 35 to 40 craft sticks (or small branches 12 to 15 cm long)
- a piece of cardboard 15 cm by 50 cm
- white glue

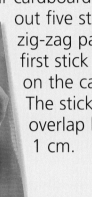

1. On your cardboard base, lay out five sticks in a zig-zag pattern. The first stick will be flat on the cardboard. The sticks should overlap by about 1 cm.

2. Add more rails to your fence one layer at a time. Always start at the same end.

3. Try it first without glue. The early settlers built fences like this so they would stand up without wire or nails. To make your fence stronger, build it again with glue. Glue the first stick to your base, and put a little glue where the sticks overlap.

The Snake Rail Fence

Two hundred years upon the clock,
  a Scotsman cleared tall trees and rock,
    plowed the land, and raised livestock,
  a house of logs—one door, no lock.
    He built a snake rail fence.

    A grandson's son got the spread;
  the old log house became a shed.
  He built a big, stone house instead
  for his young bride he soon would wed.
He fixed the snake rail fence.

My Gran grew in that house of stone,
  learned to cook and ride a roan,
    made her dresses, all hand sewn.
    At 18, married, left all she'd known.
    She missed that snake rail fence.

    Although this city's home to me,
    I think about the legacy
  of farms, of land, of *strong and free*,
  of those who shaped what I can be.
Their mark remains, still there to see,
the snake rail fence.

Farming Tools and Equipment

Early settlers used a variety of tools and equipment for farming. Some were used by hand. Some were pulled by animals.

Planting Fields

Settlers used equipment pulled by oxen or horses to work the land. A plow was used to turn over new ground.

Hand Tools

① Wide rakes were used for gathering hay.

② Hoes were used for planting and weeding.

③ Forks were used for loading hay and removing animal waste from the barn.

Animal waste, or **manure**, was spread around fruit trees, in gardens, and on fields to add nutrients to the soil.

The teeth of a harrow broke up the ground. A cultivator was used to loosen the ground and keep down weeds. The picture below shows grain being planted by hand. Later, some crops like turnips and potatoes were sown using a special planter.

Harvesting Fields

Settlers had to harvest their crops by hand. They used a scythe to cut grass and crops like wheat. A scythe had a wooden handle and a sharp, curved metal blade.

A cradle scythe cut the grain and made it fall in a pile.

Threshing the grain had two steps. First, the farmer hit the grain with a flail. A flail was made from two wooden sticks attached to each other. It knocked the grain from the stalk and loosened the outer covering of the grain kernel.

Then, the farmer tossed the grain into the air with a winnowing pan. The wind blew away the outer covering. The picture on the left shows a man winnowing grain.

Farm Vehicles

Settlers used wagons or carts for transportation. These vehicles were pulled by a horse, or by a team of horses or oxen. A team is two or more animals (or people) working together.

The most important work vehicle was the farm wagon. It was made of wood and had four strong wooden wheels. The wheels were large, to travel over rough ground and tree stumps.

Farm wagons were used for carrying people, goods, and building materials. These wagons hauled grain, wool, flour, fence rails, and lumber. Smaller, two-wheeled carts were also used for farm jobs like hauling manure or firewood.

Do ✛ Discuss ✛ Discover

1. Draw a sketch of a farm wagon or cart in your notebook.

Transportation

Sometimes settlers had to travel to the nearest village or a town farther away. They went to

- take grain or wool to the nearest mill (You will learn more about mills in another chapter.)
- buy tools and other supplies
- have equipment fixed
- sell meat, eggs, wood, and other farm products
- attend church
- visit one another

Often these trips took several hours or even days.

Early Roads

At first, there were few roads in Upper Canada. These roads were very rough, so wagons sometimes broke. They were often muddy, so wagons got stuck. In spring, roads were often so bad they could not be used.

Settlers tried to make the roads better in different ways. Logs were laid across muddy parts of the road. These were called **corduroy roads**. Wooden bridges were built over streams.

Corduroy roads were built over wet land.

When settlers got their land, they were usually required to help improve the roads. Sometimes this work did not get done because settlers were too busy on their farms.

Philip John Bainbrigge painted this picture called *Bush Farm Near Chatham* (Ontario) about 1838.

The Stagecoach

People used the stagecoach for longer trips. The stagecoach had a regular route. People paid to ride on it. It also delivered the mail.

The first stagecoach route was beside the St. Lawrence River. This road was called the King's Highway. As roads improved, stagecoaches took people to villages and towns further away from the river.

"Our progress was slow on account of the roughness of the road… to say nothing of fallen trees, big roots, mud-holes, and corduroy bridges over which you go jolt, jolt, jolt, till every bone in your body feels as if it were being dislocated.

– Catherine Parr Traill (1836)

Winter Roads and Vehicles

The roads were often better to travel on when the ground was frozen. However, storms, cold winds, and deep snow sometimes made travel difficult or impossible in winter.

Sleighs and cutters were horse-drawn vehicles with runners instead of wheels. Sleighs were used to carry heavy goods. Cutters, like the one below, were lighter sleighs that carried people.

Sometimes the wheels of the stagecoach and some wagons were replaced with runners for winter travel.

Do ⊕ Discuss ⊕ Discover

1. With a partner, look at the painting on the bottom of page 74 and find the following: log house, rail fence, tree stumps, corduroy road, farm wagon, thick forest.

2. Imagine that you are one of the settlers in this painting, returning home. Write a diary entry telling where you went and why. Remember to describe the roads and how long you travelled.

Water Transportation

Like the Aboriginal people and explorers, early settlers used the water to transport people and goods. They built rowboats and many other kinds of wooden boats. However, there were problems. Rivers and lakes froze in winter. This stopped water travel for part of the year.

Several of the rivers had rapids. Larger boats could not go through them. People and goods had to be unloaded and moved overland. Once past the rapids, the people got into another boat. The business of moving these people and goods was called forwarding. Some towns like Prescott grew because of this business.

Passengers and goods were carried by boat on canals, rivers, and lakes.

Canals

Water travel improved greatly as **canals** were built. Canals were channels or ditches that were dug and filled with water. Boats and ships used them to go around rapids and waterfalls on the rivers.

The Welland Canal was built to get around the Niagara River and Niagara Falls.

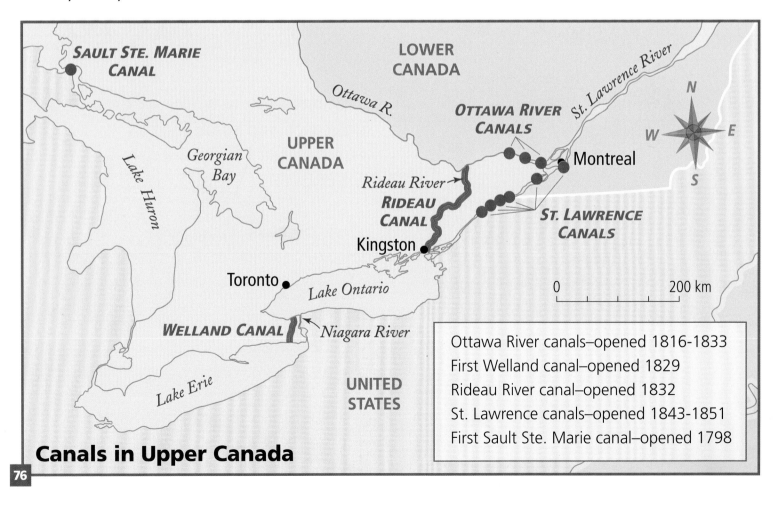

Canals in Upper Canada

SAULT STE. MARIE CANAL

LOWER CANADA

St. Lawrence River

Ottawa R.

OTTAWA RIVER CANALS

Montreal

UPPER CANADA

Georgian Bay

Lake Huron

Rideau River →

RIDEAU CANAL

ST. LAWRENCE CANALS

Kingston

Toronto

Lake Ontario

0   200 km

WELLAND CANAL

Niagara River

Lake Erie

UNITED STATES

Ottawa River canals–opened 1816-1833
First Welland canal–opened 1829
Rideau River canal–opened 1832
St. Lawrence canals–opened 1843-1851
First Sault Ste. Marie canal–opened 1798

Food

At first, early settlers hunted, fished, and gathered food just as the Aboriginal people and explorers had done. Once land was cleared, settlers grew or raised almost all of their own food. There were no grocery stores or restaurants nearby.

There were many steps needed to get this food. They had to

- plant seeds for crops, vegetables, and herbs

- harvest, thresh, and grind grain into flour

- harvest, clean, and cook fruits, vegetables, and herbs

- feed, water, and build shelter for livestock

- milk cows and gather eggs from chickens

- butcher animals for meat

From Wheat to Bread

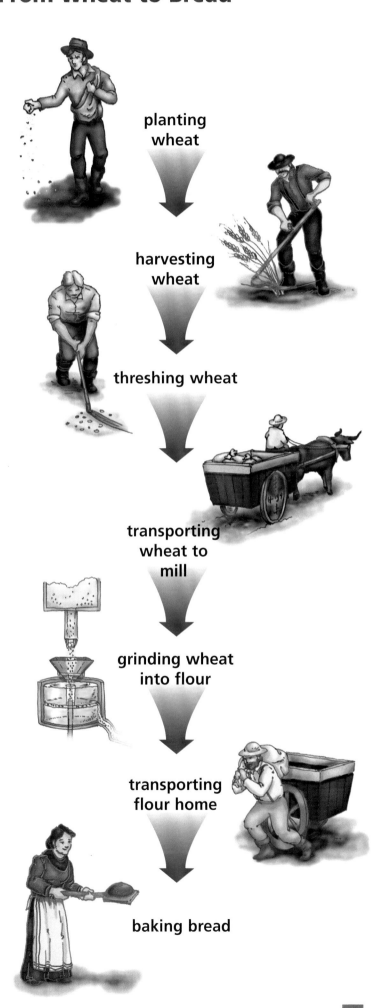

planting wheat

harvesting wheat

threshing wheat

transporting wheat to mill

grinding wheat into flour

transporting flour home

baking bread

Purchased Food

Items like salt, tea, and spices had to be bought from a village or town store. Things that came from other parts of the world were expensive and hard to get.

Settlers often made or found other products to replace hard-to-get items. For example, settlers used maple syrup instead of sugar.

Preserving Food

Settlers had to plan and work hard to have enough food to eat. Fresh milk, meat, fruit, and vegetables were only available at certain times of the year. Settlers preserved food to make it last longer. They did this in many different ways.

Preserving Food

Settlers preserved and stored food to have enough for all year. This was tricky and their efforts sometimes failed. Mice and other animals ate some of their food. Food did not always keep well. By spring, settlers often did not have enough food to eat healthy meals.

Herbs were dried.

Some vegetables were stored in a cool area below ground called a **root cellar**. Cucumbers and beets were pickled. Cabbage was sliced and packed in a barrel with salt to make sauerkraut.

Fruits and vegetables were canned or pickled.

Fruits were canned or dried. Apples were also crushed to make a drink called cider.

Meat was preserved in salt.

Meat had to be salted or smoked to preserve it. In winter, it could be kept frozen. Milk was churned into butter or made into cheese.

Using Your Learning

Understanding Concepts

1. Make a web showing the many ways that early settlers used trees. Add more parts to the web if you need them.

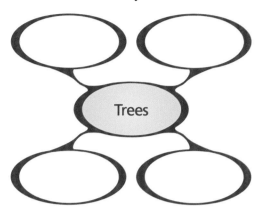

Trees

2. Fold a piece of paper into four squares. Draw pictures of four different ways that settlers travelled. Write one sentence telling which way would be your favourite and why.

3. Pick three words from the vocabulary list and add them to the *Early Settlers* New Words section in your notebook. Write a definition and make a sketch to go with each new word.

Developing Inquiry/Research and Communication Skills

4. Make up a question about farming or food that you can answer using the information in this chapter. Write your question neatly on one side of an index card. Write the answer on the other side. Give this card to your teacher.

Applying Concepts and Skills

5. a) Make a list of the foods that settlers ate and drank, and a second list of foods we eat and drink today.

   b) Choose three colours of markers. Make a word collage on a large piece of paper. Write the foods only eaten by settlers in one colour. Then, write the foods only eaten today in the second colour. Write the foods eaten in both the past and present in the third colour. Place your words on the paper in an interesting way.

Chapter 8
Family Life

Living in Upper Canada meant a lot of work for everyone. Every member of the family was expected to help. Each family member helped in different ways. Adults and children had daily jobs. In each season, there were special jobs. Sometimes, several families helped each other to do large projects.

Focus on Learning

In this chapter you will learn about
- settlers' chores
- seasonal jobs
- work done by men and boys, women and girls
- settlers working together
- time for fun

Vocabulary

chores   spinning   barn-raising
shear   work bees lacrosse
carding

Chores

Cows had to be milked every day.

Some jobs or **chores** had to be done regularly. Water was brought from the well for cooking and washing. Wood was gathered and the fire was lit. Meals were prepared and cooked.

Other jobs had to be done often. Laundry had to be washed. Clothes had to be mended and new clothing made.

Washing clothes by hand was hard work.

Livestock had to be fed and watered.

Many of these jobs took more time than they do today. Settlers could not turn on a tap to get water. There were no washing machines or microwaves. Instead, the work was done by hand. Many supplies, like candles and soap, had to be made before they could be used.

Soap was made from animal fat and a strong chemical called lye. Lye was another product made from ashes.

Gardens had to be weeded.

Seasonal Jobs

During the spring, summer, autumn, and winter, settlers had special work to do. This is similar to farming today.

Spring

- collect maple sap for syrup
- spread manure in garden and fields
- plow, harrow, and plant fields
- repair fences
- care for new piglets, lambs, and calves
- **shear** sheep for their wool; wash wool

Summer

- cut first hay crop
- build new buildings
- weed garden
- pick berries and make preserves
- harvest vegetables and early crops
- spin and dye wool

Autumn

- harvest wheat, corn, and other field crops
- gather and preserve fruits and vegetables
- smoke or salt meat; make sausages
- cut second hay crop
- plow fields
- plant winter wheat

Winter

- thresh grain
- cut trees and haul logs
- split and stack firewood
- repair and make tools, harness, utensils
- hunt, trap, and fish through the ice for food
- cut and store blocks of ice

Fire and Ice

Firewood was needed to heat the home, heat water for washing, and cook food every day. Collecting and splitting enough firewood were huge jobs.

Settlers cut ice from a lake in large blocks and stored it. They piled sawdust or straw on the ice to keep it frozen. The ice was used to keep milk and meat cool during warm weather.

Do ✛ Discuss ✛ Discover

1. Fold a paper into four squares. Open it up. Put the name of a season in each square. Draw a sketch of a seasonal chore for each season.

Everyone Helped

All family members had to help with the work. Everyone had jobs to do. For some jobs, like harvesting, the whole family worked together.

Men and Boys

Men usually worked the fields and planted the crops. They trained and drove the horses and oxen, and cared for livestock. Men built and repaired fences, buildings, and tools.

Boys helped with many of these jobs. This is the way they learned how to farm. Boys helped with chores and field work. They helped feed and clean up after the animals. They also carried in water and firewood.

Spinning

Carding and spinning wool into yarn were jobs most girls learned. Carding combed the wool fibres straight. Spinning twisted the wool into a long strand of yarn. This twist made the yarn strong. Wool was often spun using a spinning wheel.

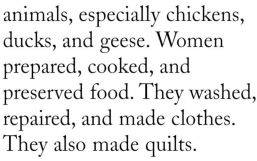

Women and Girls

Women and girls worked in the home and kept the garden. They also helped care for the animals, especially chickens, ducks, and geese. Women prepared, cooked, and preserved food. They washed, repaired, and made clothes. They also made quilts.

Girls helped their mothers with the washing and other important household tasks. They learned their mother's skills by helping. They learned to cook, knit, and sew. Women and older girls looked after and taught the children.

From Sheep to Clothing

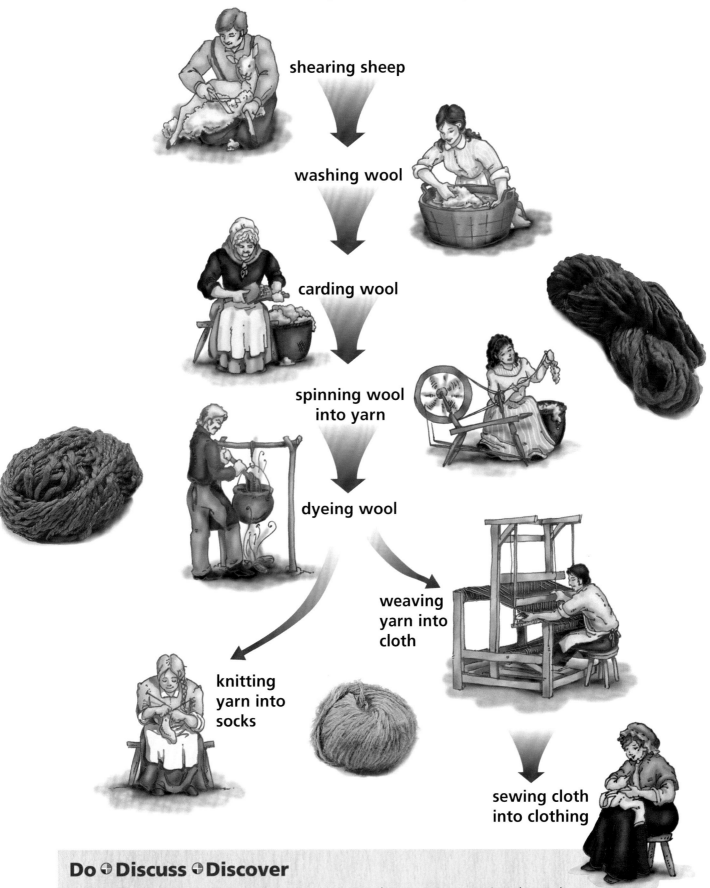

shearing sheep

washing wool

carding wool

spinning wool into yarn

dyeing wool

weaving yarn into cloth

knitting yarn into socks

sewing cloth into clothing

Do ✚ Discuss ✚ Discover

1. Try this experiment with a piece of yarn.

   a) Cut the yarn into two pieces.

   b) Untwist one piece of yarn. Try pulling it apart.

   c) Do not untwist the other piece of yarn. Try pulling it apart. Which piece was hardest to pull apart? Why?

Working Together

Sometimes families got together to help each other with large jobs. These were called work bees.

Women often worked together to make quilts. At quilting bees, they had a chance to visit with each other and hear the latest news.

Neighbours got together to build fences, chop wood, and harvest crops.

One big project was a barn-raising. It took many men to push up the strong wooden frames that became the new barn walls. Once the work was done, everyone at the bee ate and drank together.

All of the neighbours helped to put up the frame of a new barn.

Time for Fun

Settlers worked hard, but they also found time to have fun. They visited each other and celebrated special events like weddings.

Settlers enjoyed dancing to music. Some people had musical instruments, like fiddles (violins) or penny whistles. They would play for others to dance or sing.

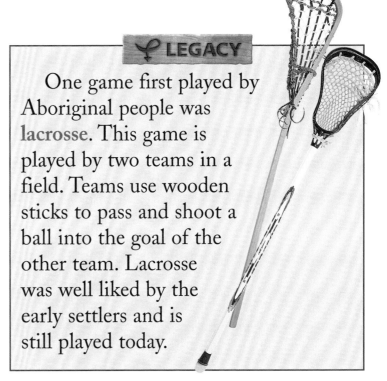

LEGACY

One game first played by Aboriginal people was **lacrosse**. This game is played by two teams in a field. Teams use wooden sticks to pass and shoot a ball into the goal of the other team. Lacrosse was well liked by the early settlers and is still played today.

Many toys and games were home made. Paper dolls, wooden puzzles, cards, and games like checkers were common. People also enjoyed collecting objects from nature.

In time, settlers were able to enjoy other activities. Watercolour painting, sketching, and making cut-paper pictures were popular.

Settlers enjoyed sports when they had time. Some winter sports were tobogganing, ice skating, horse racing, and curling. In summer, settlers played an early form of baseball.

A travelling circus or a group of actors sometimes performed in a nearby town. Picnics were also popular.

One game that children played was Blind Man's Bluff.

Both Aboriginal and settler children played with dolls.

Making a Spinner

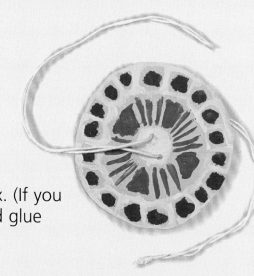

You will need:

- cereal box or heavy paper
- pencil and markers or paints
- glue stick or glue
- scissors and string

1. Cut a circle about 15 cm across from the cereal box. (If you are using paper, cut 3 or 4 circles the same size and glue them together.)

2. Make patterns on one or both sides of the circle.

3. Colour your patterns.

4. Find the centre of your circle and make two small holes about 0.75 cm on each side of the centre.

5. Cut two pieces of string, each about 50 cm long.

6. Thread one end of each string through a hole.

7. Tie the strings together at both ends.

8. Hold one end in each hand, keeping the string tight. Ask a friend to twist the strings by turning the spinner.

9. Have your friend let go. Pull your hands gently apart. Your spinner should begin to spin! Relax your hands a little to let it wind the other way, then pull again to get your spinner to keep spinning.

Tops and other spinning toys were popular. Paper spinners were called thaumatropes. Today, spinners can also be made from large buttons.

Using Your Learning

Understanding Concepts

1. Imagine that you are an early settler. Write two sentences that rhyme (called a rhyming couplet) about a daily or seasonal chore. For example:

   Cows are milked every day;
   We get milk and cheese that way.
   or
   Wash the clothes in a wooden tub;
   With lye soap you'll have to scrub.

   Practise reading your couplet aloud.

2. Pick three words from the vocabulary list and add them to the *Early Settlers* New Words section in your notebook. Write a definition and make a sketch to go with each new word.

Developing Inquiry/Research and Communication Skills

3. Make up a question about the family life of settlers that you can answer using the information in this chapter. Write your question neatly on one side of an index card. Write the answer on the other side. Give this card to your teacher.

Applying Concepts and Skills

4. Settlers had to store ice to keep their food cool in warm weather. What materials in your environment will keep a small block of ice from melting for the longest time? Try this experiment:

   a) Choose different materials.

   b) Wrap one ice cube in each material.

   c) Record the time each ice cube takes to melt.

   d) As a class, compare results.

5. Imagine your settler family is having a work bee in early summer. Decide on the food and drinks you will serve when the work is done.

6. Make a Venn diagram to compare the chores that settler children did with the chores that you do. Show your Venn diagram to a partner and discuss whether or not you would like to be a part of a settler's family.

Chapter 9
Early Villages

Before long, several small villages began in Upper Canada. Villages often started near a lake or river. Mills and other businesses needed a good water supply. Mills used water power to run machinery. These mills did important jobs for early settlers. Sawmills cut logs into boards, and grist mills made flour from grain.

Focus on Learning

In this chapter you will learn about
- the first villages in Upper Canada
- the growth of villages
- water power
- the sawmill
- the grist mill

Vocabulary

mills	turbine
sawmills	driveshaft
grist mills	lumber
waterwheel	millstones

A Village Begins

Most villages started near water. People got drinking water and fish from lakes and rivers. Travelling was easier by water than by land. So was transporting goods.

Many businesses used water to make things. For example, water was used to tan leather and to make bricks.

Mills used water to run machinery. Early settlers knew how to build mills and use water power when they came to Upper Canada. Often a new village would start around one of these mills.

The St. Lawrence River and the Great Lakes were very important to early settlers in Upper Canada. Most of the earliest villages began near these bodies of water.

The city of Toronto began as a small village called York on the shore of Lake Ontario. This picture of York was made in 1803.

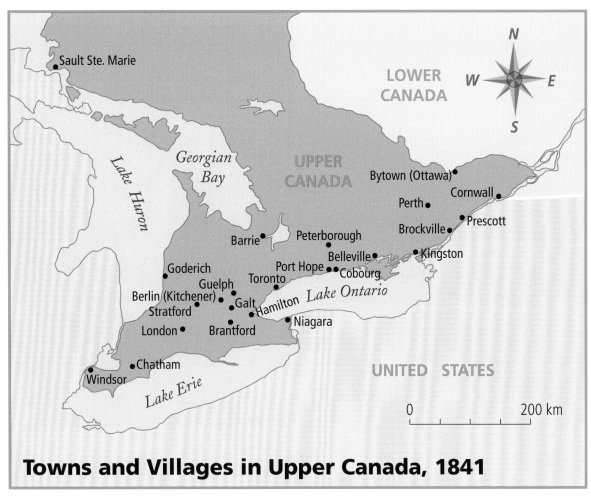

Towns and Villages in Upper Canada, 1841

The Village Grows

Once a mill was built, settlers went to it to get work done. Some settlers got jobs at the mill. New settlers moved to the area because of the mill.

Other mills were often built nearby. New businesses started up. They served the needs of mill owners, workers, and farmers who came to the mills. These businesses and jobs attracted more people to live there. Soon there were enough people that a church and school were needed. Before long, a village was born!

Other Villages

Some villages began when settlers made their homes near forts. These settlers grew food for the soldiers. Over time, these settled areas grew into villages, and then into towns. Some of these towns became large cities. For example, Fort Cataraqui, an early French fort, is now the city of Kingston.

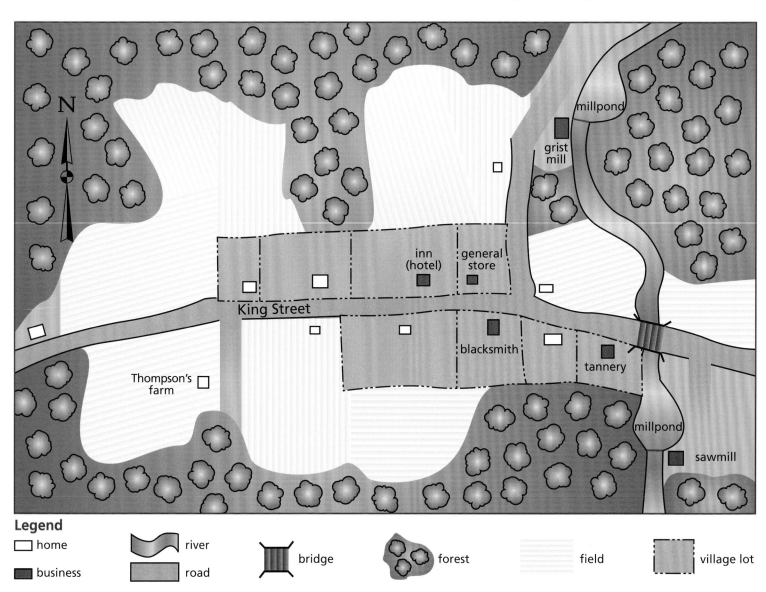

Legend

☐ home   〰 river   ⊟ bridge   🌳 forest   field   village lot

■ business   road

Water Power

Early mills used water to run the machines in the mill. To use this water, mill owners often built a dam across a river or stream. This dam held back the water in a millpond until it was needed.

Mills only ran when there was work to do and there was enough water. This was usually in the spring and summer.

This millpond holds water used by the grist mill at Upper Canada Village.

1 The gate holding back the water was opened.

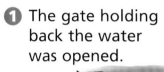

2 Water flowed into the mill through a ditch or wooden channel called a raceway.

3 Water flowed onto a large wooden **waterwheel** or through a **turbine**, causing it to turn.

A turbine is a type of waterwheel. Turbines were made of iron rather than wood.

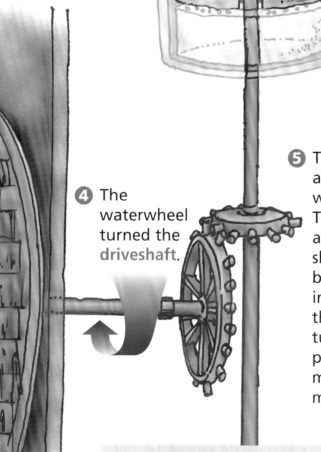

4 The waterwheel turned the **driveshaft**.

5 The driveshaft was attached to round wooden gears. These were attached to other shafts, pulleys, belts, and elevators in the mill. When the driveshaft turned, these parts moved and made all of the machinery run.

Do ✛ Discuss ✛ Discover

1. Re-read pages 91 to 93. Design a web that shows reasons why lakes and rivers were important to early settlers.

The Sawmill

Often, the first mill to be built was the sawmill. The sawmill cut logs into different sizes of square timber, planks, and boards. These pieces of cut wood are called lumber. Some sawmills also cut wooden shingles for roofs.

Sawmills were often built quickly out of rough boards.

Settlers' homes, barns, and many other buildings were built from wood. It was slow, hard work to cut this wood with hand tools. Sawmills were able to saw lumber more easily and much faster.

Settlers cut trees in winter. They brought the logs to the sawmill in spring. The lumber they took home was sawn from their own logs.

Spring was a busy time. Some sawmills ran 24 hours a day. Skilled workers in the sawmill were called sawyers.

The sawyer was usually paid in lumber instead of money. Half the lumber that was sawn became his to sell later.

Sawmills had a long sawblade with large teeth. The blade ran up and down. Water power was used to make the sawblade move. Water power was also used to move the log towards the sawblade.

Round logs were first cut square.

Squared logs were cut into planks and thinner boards in the sawmill.

The Grist Mill

Grain that was going to be, or had been, ground into small pieces was called grist. Settlers took their wheat to a grist mill to be made into flour. Two heavy stone wheels called **millstones** were used to grind their wheat into flour.

Some grist mills made only whole wheat flour. Whole wheat flour was made from the whole kernel of the wheat. White flour came from one part of the kernel. It was more expensive, but most people preferred to use it.

Millstones had special grooves cut into them to help grind flour.

The miller was usually paid in wheat. He got 1/12 of the weight of the wheat a farmer brought. Later, he sold or traded the flour he made from it.

2 Grain was poured through a hole in the middle of the top millstone.

1 Moving water turned the waterwheel, which turned the driveshaft and powered the mill's machines.

4 An elevator carried the whole wheat flour to a machine called a bolter.

5 The bolter separated the white flour from the other parts of the wheat kernel.

3 The top stone turned. It forced wheat between the stones and ground it into flour.

Do ⊕ Discuss ⊕ Discover

1. In your notebook, draw your own diagram of how the grist mill worked. Be sure to include labels.

Diary of Alex Bell, 1840

January

11 fine day

20 fresh fish for dinner; Sarah making shirts

21 threshed wheat

27 hauled logs to road

February

11 mended the harness; very cold day; Sarah making pies

21 David cut his foot chopping wood

24 took wheat to mill

March

10 hauled 4 oak logs to Dixon's mill

17 snow nearly gone, but roads bad

22 tapped 10 trees, no sugar yet

30 fixed David's boots; foot healing well

April

7 hard frost last night; plowed in the afternoon

15 hauled manure to garden; men working in sawmill night & day

22 planted 8 apple trees

May

4 sowed 6 bushels of peas

6 sowed Scotch wheat

15 Sarah sowed a few seeds in the garden

18 Sarah mending shirts

20 planted potatoes and corn

24 Sarah turned house upside down, cleaning

June

5 went to Brockville

7 fixed fence

12 Sarah made a cheese

30 weather hot; Sarah called on Mrs. Bissell who has a broken arm

July

6 ground very dry

14 first raspberries today; rain yesterday

24 brought in hay

August

3 went to Brockville; bought a scythe

17 began to cut the wheat

23 cut the oats

September

1 plowed

8 brought in peas and flax

20 took horses for shoes

October

1 Sarah making pumpkin pies

14 fixed floor in woodshed

19 Sarah at sewing bee

25 threshed wheat; 1 foot of snow has fallen; very bad roads

November

4 Sarah finished her dress

15 cleaned the dried peas

21 roads rough

29 helped Mr. Davis thresh

December

2 Sarah making trousers

11 finished nailing boards on woodshed; letter from William, all well

14 killed 1 sheep and 2 pigs

18 cold, no sleighing

Using Your Learning

Understanding Concepts

1. In your own words, explain why mills were an important part of early villages. What were the first types of mills, and what jobs did they do for settlers?

2. Use the map on page 91 to help you label the towns and villages of Upper Canada on a blank map. Put the map in your notebook.

3. Pick three words from the vocabulary list and add them to the *Early Settlers* New Words section in your notebook. Write a definition and make a sketch to go with each new word.

Developing Inquiry/Research and Communication Skills

4. Make up a question about mills that you can answer using the information in this chapter. Write your question neatly on one side of an index card. Write the answer on the other side. Give this card to your teacher.

5. Diaries are an important source of information about life in the past. Re-read Diary of Alex Bell, 1840, and answer these questions. Remember to give proof for each answer from the diary:

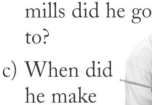

a) What jobs did men and women do?

b) What types of mills did he go to?

c) When did he make these trips?

d) What work did he do in March?

e) What were the roads like in November?

Applying Concepts and Skills

6. Keep a diary for one week. List what you and your family do each day and any special activities. Look at your finished diary. Are there any similarities between your diary and Alex Bell's diary? What information about life today would your diary give to someone reading it?

Chapter 10
Village Trades

Early settlers had to make and repair many things themselves. As villages grew, settlers could get help from different tradespeople. These people had special knowledge and skills working with iron, wood, and leather. They made and repaired many things for settlers.

Focus on Learning

In this chapter you will learn about
- tradespeople and their tools
- the blacksmith
- primary and secondary sources of information
- woodworkers
- leather workers
- other tradespeople

Vocabulary

blacksmith   coopers
carpenter   harness-makers

Trades

A trade is a special set of skills. Tradespeople use specific tools and materials. They use their knowledge and skills to make or fix things. They usually work with their hands.

This woodworker is using a lathe to make a table leg.

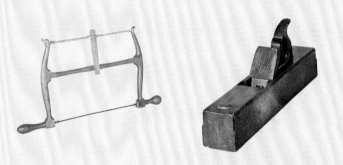
Today, plumbers, electricians, and auto mechanics are some examples of tradespeople. In the past, different trades were important.

Some early settlers had the skills and knowledge of a special trade before they came to Upper Canada. Others learned their skills after they arrived.

Tradespeople had several kinds of hand saws for different jobs. They had to care for their tools and keep them sharp.

Do ✛ Discuss ✛ Discover

1. Name five trades that exist today. List one special tool or skill for each.

The Blacksmith

One of the most important tradespeople was the blacksmith. Blacksmiths worked and shaped iron. Hot iron bent more easily. They used a hot fire called a forge to heat the iron. They pumped a bellows to blow air into the forge. This made it burn hotter.

A blacksmith held the piece of hot iron with tongs. He laid it on his anvil and hit it with a heavy hammer to shape it. Blacksmiths also had other tools for cutting and shaping iron.

Iron Working

Blacksmiths made and repaired many different iron tools and objects. They made many of their own tools. They also made shoes for horses, door latches, hooks, spikes, and hinges. They repaired farm and mill equipment. Many blacksmiths made parts and repaired wagons.

Horseshoes

Blacksmiths spent much of their time making horseshoes and working on horses' feet. Horses' hooves are like our toenails. They need to be trimmed.

When horses or oxen worked on hard, dry roads, their hooves could get chipped or cracked. Shoes helped to protect their feet. In time, horseshoes wore out and new ones had to be made.

Blacksmiths sometimes made special shoes to fix the way a horse was walking. They also made shoes for different weather conditions. Winter shoes had special points on them. This helped horses grip better on icy roads.

Metal horseshoes protected the horse's feet. The blacksmith pulled them off to trim the horse's hooves. Then, he nailed them back on with special nails.

Primary and Secondary Sources of Information

There are two main sources of information we use to learn about the past. We use information from people who did or saw things themselves in the past. These are called **primary sources**. These sources often give us important details about life in the past.

Information from people who have studied the past but did not live at that time are **secondary sources**.

Some examples of primary sources are personal diaries, letters, business records, and photographs. Some examples of secondary sources are books, models, and CD-ROMs.

Many tradespeople kept track of their work by writing in a daybook. The photograph shows a page from a blacksmith's daybook. Parts of this page have been put in the chart below. The information in brackets has been added to help you.

Customer	Work Done	Price
Richard Foxton	2 shoes set [put back on]	1/3 [1 shilling and 3 pence = 25 cents]
J. Lamb	one shoe set [put back on]	7 1/2 [7 1/2 pence = 12 cents]
Wm. [William] Morrison	2 shoes set [put back on]	1/3 [1 shilling and 3 pence = 25 cents]
Thomas Johnson	one tire set [iron band put on wooden wagon wheel]	3/0 [3 shillings = 60 cents]

Do ✚ Discuss ✚ Discover

1. Use information from this page to answer these questions:

   a) When was the daybook written?

   b) What kinds of jobs did a blacksmith do?

   c) What was the most common job?

   d) What did it cost to have a horseshoe put on?

2. Is the daybook a primary or a secondary source? Is the illustration on page 98 a primary or secondary source? Explain your answers.

Woodworkers

Wood was an important building material. It was easy to get and cheap compared to many other materials.

Several tradespeople built and repaired objects using wood. Woodworkers used saws for cutting boards. They used hand planes for smoothing, shaping, and cutting grooves. They had other tools for measuring, splitting, smoothing, making holes, and fastening pieces together. The photographs on page 99 show many woodworking tools.

Woodworkers made chairs by hand. This piece was for a chair back.

Carpenter

I build wooden buildings. I only need a few tools to measure, cut, and put together the pieces of wood for the frame of the building. Then, I cover it with boards.

Remember the carpenter's rule: measure twice and cut once!

Joiner

I am very good at making different kinds of joints that join pieces of wood together. That's why they call me a joiner!

I often help carpenters by making the doors and window frames that go into their buildings.

Cabinetmaker

I learned my skills over several years. I make chairs, tables, and other furniture for people's homes. Most are made from wood grown here, which I buy from the sawmill.

I can paint, stencil, or polish this furniture until it shines! I have many hand tools, some of which I made myself.

Cooper

Coopers like me make wooden buckets and washtubs. We also make barrels to transport goods. Barrels are made from curved pieces of wood held together by wooden or metal hoops.

My barrels are for dry goods like ashes, flour, or apples. Some coopers make waterproof barrels for cider and other liquids. They are made carefully so they will not leak.

Leather Workers

Leather was another important material for early settlers. They used leather to make shoes. It was also used on the farm. Shoemakers and harness-makers were tradespeople who worked with leather. Harness-makers made the straps horses wore to do work.

Leather was made in a tannery. Tanneries were businesses where animal skins were turned into leather. Tanners soaked skins in a mixture of oak bark and water to make leather.

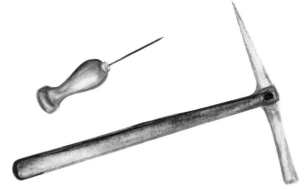

A leather worker's awl was used to punch holes in leather. This small hammer was a saddler's tool. Saddlers made leather saddles for horses.

Shoemaker

I make shoes and boots from leather. I have a sharp knife to cut it. I use an awl to make holes before I sew the pieces of leather together with linen thread.

I shape these pieces over a wooden form called a last. I have different sizes of lasts because people have different sizes of feet! I use a hammer and wooden pegs or nails to attach the shoe's sole and heel pieces.

A shoemaker used a wooden last as a form for making shoes and boots.

Sometimes a shoemaker came to a settler's home and stayed until everyone had a new pair of shoes.

Harness-maker

I make harness for horses. I sew all the leather straps they wear. I stuff and sew the collar that fits on their necks.

I work with knives, awls, and linen thread like the shoemaker does. I also have a wooden clamp. I use it to hold the leather pieces I am sewing together.

A horse's harness straps had to be strong for pulling heavy loads.

Other Tradespeople

Villages and towns sometimes had other tradespeople living in them.

The baker mixed the dough by hand in a large wooden dough box.

Bread was baked in a brick oven heated with a wood fire. Then, it was set to cool.

The tinsmith's shop was both a work area and a store. The shelves displayed his products.

Baker

Most people in the village don't need to buy my bread! They bake their own at home.

I sell my bread to the hotel, which makes meals for travellers in town. I also sell to soldiers and labourers. They live in work camps while they work on the new canal and railroad nearby.

Tinsmith

I make all sorts of useful items like pails, kitchen utensils, candle holders, and lanterns. I use a thin shiny metal called tin-plate that has to be shipped from Britain.

One way I join the pieces together is with solder. Solder is a melted metal that acts like glue. I heat it until it melts. It flows into the joints and hardens. I roll the rims of pails around a wire to make them stronger.

Do ✛ Discuss ✛ Discover

1. Choose one of the tradespeople in this chapter and make a "Who am I?" riddle. Fold a piece of paper in half. Write clues about tools, materials, and products on the outside. Write the answer on the inside.

Using Your Learning

Understanding Concepts

1. What materials did different tradespeople use? Try to find examples of things made from these materials in your home. List what you found.

2. Pick one word from the vocabulary list and add it to the *Early Settlers* New Words section in your notebook. Write a definition and make a sketch to go with this new word.

Developing Inquiry/Research and Communication Skills

3. Why was a blacksmith called a "blacksmith"? Check the website: www.word-detective.com/082498.html or do your own Internet search for "blacksmith"+"meaning."

4. Make up a question about village trades that you can answer using the information in this chapter. Write your question neatly on one side of an index card. Write the answer on the other side. Give this card to your teacher.

5. Learn more about tradespeople in the past by visiting a local museum or the website www.uppercanada village.com. Click on "Tour the Village."

Applying Concepts and Skills

6. Choose two tradespeople described in this chapter. In a chart, compare the tools they used with tools used today in the same trades.

7. In your home, find two primary sources of information about your family. With your parents' permission, bring one of these sources to school. Show your item to your class and tell them what information it reveals about your family.

Chapter 11
Village Life

As villages grew, there were more businesses, new buildings, and special activities. Even the smallest village usually had at least one store, a school, and a church. There was often a doctor. Community celebrations were also part of village life.

Focus on Learning

In this chapter you will learn about
- how villages grew
- the general store
- the common school
- early churches
- early settlers' health
- special celebrations

Vocabulary

general store
merchants
accounts

copybook
celebrate
fall fair

The Village Grows

Many villages grew quickly as the population of Upper Canada increased. More businesses were started. New buildings were added. More activities took place in these villages. In time, some villages became towns and even large cities.

Compare the village plan below with the plan on page 92. Now there is less forest around the village. There are more fields. There are more homes and businesses. The streets divide the village into square blocks. What other changes do you see?

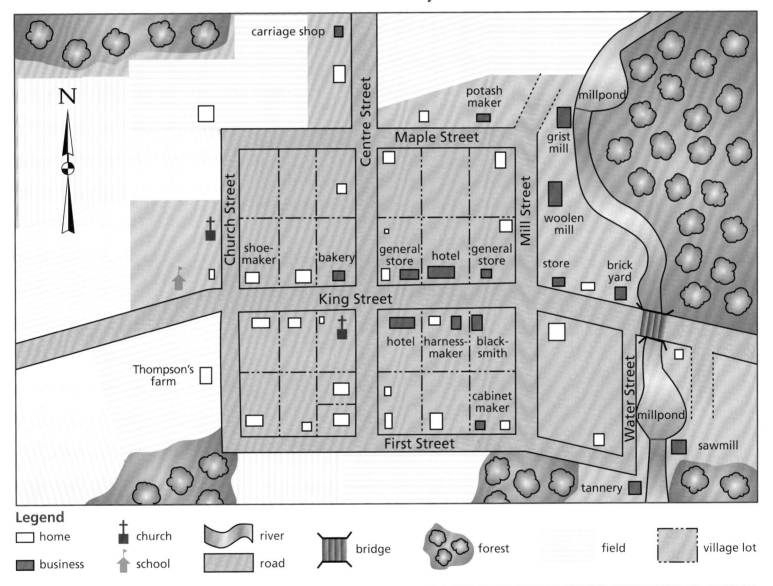

Legend

☐ home ✝ church ∿ river ⊟ bridge 🌳 forest field village lot

◼ business ⬆ school road

Do ⊕ Discuss ⊕ Discover

1. a) Write two questions that can be answered using this map of an imaginary village. Two examples are "Where does the shoemaker live?" and "How do you get from the school to the cabinetmaker's shop?"

b) Exchange questions with a partner and check each others' answers.

c) With your partner, discuss which parts of the map were used for each question and answer. For help, look at page 5 on Map Reading.

The General Store

A small village usually had only one or two stores. They had a wide range of things for sale. This type of store was known as a general store.

Village merchants ordered their goods from larger cities like Montreal. These goods mostly came by boat. Many merchants owned their own dock where the boats unloaded their goods.

The rivers and lakes froze in winter, so shipments stopped until spring. After railways were built, merchants could get goods year round.

Most general stores sold tea, spices, sugar, tobacco, dishes, nails, bolts, hinges, axes, rope, cloth, medicines, and candy. Many goods were sold by weight.

Selling Goods

Merchants were store owners. They sent away for goods that settlers could not make for themselves. They sold goods to people in the village and surrounding area. The general store was often the post office. Mail came by steamboat or stagecoach to the post office.

How People Paid

In Upper Canada there was very little paper money and few coins. Customers of a general store often paid with farm products or work instead of cash. Merchants often accepted wood, eggs, or even a day's work.

Settlers sometimes paid with homemade goods like cheese and homespun wool.

Money

No Canadian dollars and coins were made until 1858. Settlers in Upper Canada used British money called pounds, shillings, and pence. Some American money was also used. Banks and other businesses often used written notes and bank tokens like these as money.

Aboriginal people living in nearby villages visited to get supplies and to sell fish and other products.

Merchants kept written records called **accounts**. They wrote down the customer's name, what was sold, the price, and what the customer was able to pay. When settlers got the money, they paid what they still owed. This was called "settling your account."

Merchants kept their accounts up-to-date.

Do ✛ Discuss ✛ Discover

1. Imagine you are an early settler. With a partner, discuss what things you would probably need to buy. How might you pay?

The Common School

At first, there were no schools. Children learned at home. Some parents thought the work at home was more important than school. They did not have to send their children to school.

As villages grew, schools were built. Most villages had a "common school."

These schools were simple log buildings with only one room. Students worked through lesson books instead of being in grades. They also helped with school chores like bringing in firewood.

Students did most of their work with chalk on small slate boards. These were like small blackboards. Paper was expensive and only used for their good copy.

Pens were made out of a goose feather. The end was cut to make a point. Students dipped this end into a small bottle of ink. These pens were called quill pens.

The art of writing neatly with a pen was thought to be important. This skill was called "penmanship." Students could buy a copybook from the general store to practise their writing.

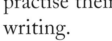

Teaching School

Teachers taught children of different ages together in one room. Their students were expected to learn most things by repeating them from memory. Teachers taught reading, writing, arithmetic, discipline, and proper behaviour. Some teachers were as young as 14 years old!

Making a Copybook

You will need:

- 3 to 5 sheets of plain 8½" x 14" paper
- 1 piece of light-weight bristol board 23 cm x 28 cm for cover
- nail, hammer, and wooden board
- tapestry (blunt) needle and string

1. Fold your paper and cover in half.

2. Make 5 dots on the centre fold.

3. Put the board underneath the book and use the nail and hammer to make 5 holes on your dots.*

4. Thread the string on the needle. Pull half of the string through the bottom hole. Keep hold of the other end so it doesn't pull through the hole. Continue to sew your book by pulling the needle through each hole.

5. Thread the other half of the string on the needle. Sew to the top again, starting from the other side.

6. Tie the two string ends together near the top hole.

7. Put a title on your copybook.

   For example: "This Copybook belongs to..."

   Now it's ready to use!

*Be careful with tools! Your teacher can help you.

Church

Most people thought it was important to attend church. At first, there were few churches. People read the Bible at home. They also met in other buildings such as the school.

Usually it was not long before money was raised to build a church. Many of these early churches were built out of log or stone.

Most villages had to share a minister or priest with at least one other village. The minister or priest travelled between them.

Other religious speakers also travelled from village to village to preach and share their beliefs.

Health

Many settlers got sick or were injured at some time during their lives. Settlers worked with sharp tools and near open fires. Sometimes there were serious accidents. People were cut or burned.

Settlers also worked with large animals. Sometimes they were bitten, kicked, or thrown off their horses. In winter, people could get frostbite. Settlers also got ill from diseases like measles, typhus, and cholera.

The Doctor

At first, there were few doctors and no hospitals in Upper Canada. Settlers were cared for at home.

Doctors did not always understand the reasons for sickness. Sometimes their treatments did not help. Settlers often tried a home remedy or a medicine from the general store first, before they sent for a doctor.

Women usually helped each other have babies. They only sent for the doctor when it seemed absolutely necessary.

Treating Sickness

The doctor treated people for pain and other signs of diseases. They used many different medicines. Doctors had tools for helping mothers have babies. They also had tools for removing sore or rotten teeth.

This medicine chest holds glass bottles and has drawers for different medicines.

Visiting and Celebrations

Settlers came together to visit and **celebrate** at different times of the year. They joined in special activities in honour of a special time or person.

Often, settlers visited and celebrated in a nearby village. They met at church and in the general store, the blacksmith's shop, and the local mill. They shared news with neighbours.

In the spring and the fall, there were special community events.

The Queen's Birthday

Queen Victoria's birthday was celebrated on May 24. It was a time for settlers to celebrate the arrival of spring. They also showed their respect and admiration for their queen. Victoria Day celebrations often included speeches, a parade, athletic games, and military demonstrations.

The Fall Fair

An important event in the fall was the Agricultural Exhibition, or **fall fair**. Settlers came together to celebrate a successful harvest. It was also a time for friendly competition. Settlers entered animals, vegetables, and home-made goods. These were judged, and prizes were given for the best entries.

♀ LEGACY

Fall fairs are still held in many towns and villages all over Ontario.

A prize-winning chicken gets a ribbon at the fair in Georgetown, Ontario.

113

Reader's Theatre: At the Fair

Cow: I do say, it's my old friend Mr. Canadian! Can it be a year since our last fall fair?

Horse: Mrs. Shorthorn! A full year it is. How do you do, neighhh-bour?

Cow: Very well, indeed. The cheese my family made from my milk won first prize again this year. Who is that curly headed fellow with you?

Horse: Mr. Cotswold has recently moved here from Britain.

Cow: How do you do, Mr. Cotswold?

Sheep: Not too baa-dly, thank you. My mistress took first place for her spun yarn. The shawl she knit won second. She told the other ladies that my wool is wonderful to work with.

Cow: Really? Did I mention that my butter won a prize? The judge asked my mistress if he could take home the rest of the crock.

Pig: To eat it?

Cow: Mr. Berkshire! How good to see you again. I see eating is still your favourite thing to do.

Pig: Is it almost supper?

Horse: I'm sure we shall all be going home soon, Mr. Berkshire. It has been a full day for everyone. After the plowing matches, I saw my family walk over to the stage.

They listened to the speeches and the fiddle music. Everyone watched the spelling bee.

Cow: The children have not been this excited since Christmas!

Horse: Mr. Berkshire, your master grows a big garden. How did he do in the vegetable competition?

Pig: Umm, not so well this year.

Horse: Why not? His carrots are known to be the best.

Pig: True, but when his back was turned...

Cow: What? What happened?

Pig: I ate them!

Do ⊕ Discuss ⊕ Discover

1. What are the names of the animals? Can you guess why?

Using Your Learning

Understanding Concepts

1. Review pages 108 and 109 and answer the following questions in your notebook in a short paragraph. What did merchants sell? How did they keep track of their sales? How did settlers pay?

2. Pick two words from the vocabulary list and add them to the *Early Settlers* New Words section in your notebook. Write a definition and make a sketch to go with each new word.

Developing Inquiry/Research and Communication Skills

3. Make up a question about village life that you can answer using the information in this chapter. Write your question neatly on one side of an index card. Write the answer on the other side. Give this card to your teacher.

4. Construct a model of an early settler home, business, church, or school. As a class, put your models together to make a model village.

5. Look on the Internet to find information about the Canadian Horse, one of our newest Canadian symbols.

Write three facts about this breed. Check the following websites: www.imh.org/imh/bw/canada.html (click on "Breed Characteristics"); or www.canadianhorse.net (click on "Breed history").

Applying Concepts and Skills

6. Write a short paragraph comparing the lives of early settlers to life today. Choose school, health, or shopping as your topic.

7. Choose a favourite poem or saying. Write it as neatly as possible to demonstrate your "penmanship."

8. Look back at pages 2 and 3. With a partner, identify the people and activities in each part of the picture. List the order in which these things happened in Upper Canada.

Chapter 12
Changing Times

Between 1840 and 1867, life in Upper Canada changed in important ways. The number of settlers grew tremendously. Several large towns and cities were established. Better types of livestock, crops, and equipment were available. Farms became more successful. Travel was easier and faster. There was also a new system of communication.

Focus on Learning

In this chapter you will learn about
- changes in farming
- new machines and jobs for settlers
- changes in transportation

Vocabulary

factories   steam engines

Changes on the Farm

Major changes helped settlers to be more successful farmers. New types of crops and livestock were developed. They were better matched to the climate in Upper Canada. Farmers could grow more and produce better products.

Farmers were able to get more horse-drawn equipment. They could buy swathers and mowers to cut down grain and hay. There were rakes to gather the hay in rows. This made field work much faster. Crops were less likely to get damaged by bad weather.

Threshing machines replaced flails and winnowing pans.

Once the crop was at the barn, machines for threshing separated out the kernels of grain. Horses walked on a treadmill to provide power. (Find the picture of a treadmill on page 116.)

In time, these changes helped settlers to make more money. They built larger, nicer homes. People could buy and enjoy more things. Some settlers bought more land and had larger farms. Others started new businesses.

The buck-eye mower made haying faster.

Red Fife Wheat

Red Fife Wheat was one new crop. It was developed by David Fife, a farmer near Peterborough. He experimented with seeds that first came from Eastern Europe. By 1860, Red Fife was the most popular type of wheat grown in Upper Canada.

Cheese factories produced cheese for sale from farmers' extra milk.

New Machines

New machines also changed life in Upper Canada. Iron turbines replaced many wooden waterwheels. Turbines gave mills more power.

Sawmills began to use faster circular saws. Machines in woollen mills carded wool, spun yarn, and wove cloth. They worked many times faster than settlers could at home. Large mills that could do many different jobs were called factories.

Woollen mills produced finished products as well as wool yarn.

This machine is getting wool ready to be carded.

Steam engines allowed mills and factories to run when there was not enough water for a turbine. Water was heated in a boiler to make steam. The steam moved the parts of the engine and provided power to the mill.

New Jobs

The roles of some men, women, and children also changed. Farmers had helped out at the mill for part of the year. Now, mills could run all year. They hired some men as full-time mill workers.

Some women and children were also hired to work in mills and factories. They worked long hours and were paid less than men.

Working in Factories

With steam power and new machines, factories could produce more than ever before. This meant new and different jobs were available. Workers were needed. Some jobs needed more skills than others. Factory workers had to be quick and careful. Mistakes often meant losing money.

Changes in Transportation

Steamboats changed water travel. They did not need a strong wind to move, like sailing ships did. People and goods could travel more quickly.

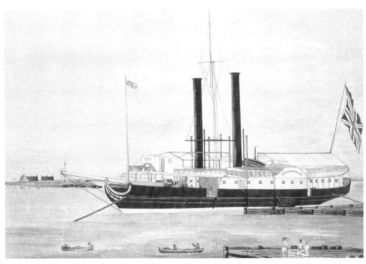

The steamboat "Great Britain" carried passengers and goods on Lake Ontario in 1839.

Steamboats were driven by steam engines attached to large paddlewheels or propellers. To make steam in the boiler, these boats burned a lot of wood. Sometimes the boilers exploded from the pressure.

This steam locomotive ran on the Grand Trunk Railway near Montreal.

By the mid-1850s, a new railway system made it easier and faster to travel in Upper Canada. The railway also used steam power. It was expensive, but it ran year-round.

The Telegraph

The invention of the telegraph was an important change in communication. The telegraph sent signals through a wire. News could travel much more quickly than before. By 1866, an underwater cable connected Newfoundland to Ireland. Messages sent to and from Europe took minutes instead of weeks.

A Different Place

In 1867, Upper Canada was a different place. It became part of a new country called Canada.

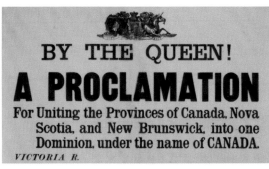

There were only four provinces when Canada was first formed.

Yet it was a place with many memories and a history. The Aboriginal people who lived in Upper Canada started us on this path. Explorers, fur traders, and soldiers made their mark. The Loyalists and many more immigrant families from the American colonies, Britain, and other countries came. They worked hard and made new homes. Over time, people's knowledge, beliefs, skills and effort changed Upper Canada.

In 1867, the Union Jack was the flag of Canada.

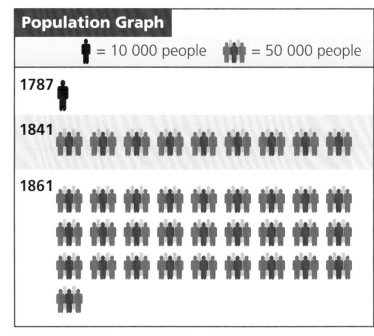

Population Graph

👤 = 10 000 people 👥 = 50 000 people

| 1787 |
| 1841 |
| 1861 |

In 1871, four years after Canada became a country, there were more than 2 600 000 people in Upper Canada. Almost all non-Aboriginal people had come from northern Europe or the United States. At this time, there were almost no people from Asia, Africa, southern Europe, South America, or Australia.

Today

How we live in Canada today is different from life in Upper Canada in many ways. Yet our lives are linked through time and place to those of the Aboriginal people and early settlers.

Today, Toronto looks very different from the picture of the village of York on page 91.

Celebrating Your Learning

As a class, hold an Early Settlers Fair to celebrate your learning. Your fair can include any or all of the following:

1. Take part in a spelling bee using the vocabulary words you have learned in each chapter. Nothing like a little friendly competition!

2. Enter a sample of your "penmanship."

3. Enter your own writing about early settlers in the fair. This might include a diary entry, historic quotation, poem, or story that you prepare and write by hand.

4. Practise and perform a short reading or poem. Repeat it from memory, just like the settlers' children did at their school.

5. With three friends, perform the Reader's Theatre: At the Fair, found on page 114.

6. Display your favourite hands-on project as an entry in the fair.

7. Make and enter a model of a waterwheel. Extra points if it works!

8. Enter a diorama or model of something about the lives of Aboriginal people or early settlers. Some ideas include a longhouse, wigwam, settler's shanty, blacksmith's shop, farm wagon, or steamboat.

For more fun, you might want to serve a food that Aboriginal people or early settlers ate. And don't forget the fiddle music!

Glossary

A

Aboriginal people—people living in a place long before others came there

accounts—written records of what people bought and paid for in a store

acre—a measured area of land equal to 4047 square metres

Anishinabe—a group of Algonquian-speaking Aboriginal people (also called Ojibwa)

awl—a pointed tool for making holes in leather so pieces could be sewn together

B

barn-raising—many neighbours working together to raise the wooden frames for a barn's walls

bateaux—flat-bottomed boats that were pointed at each end

blacksmith—a tradesperson who made and repaired iron objects such as horseshoes

C

canals—channels or ditches dug and filled with water for boats and ships to go around rapids and waterfalls on a river

carding—combing woolen fibres straight before they were spun into yarn

carpenter—a tradesperson who builds wooden buildings

celebrate—to take part in activities in honour of a special time or person

ceremonies—special activities held before or after an important event

cholera—a serious disease spread by bacteria in dirty water

chores—small jobs that are done regularly

clan—a group of families who were related to each other

clearing land—removing trees from land to make room for fields or buildings

climate—the average weather of a place over a long time

colonies—areas of land that were governed by another country

contagious—easily spread from one person to another

cooper—a tradesperson who built wooden barrels, tubs, and buckets

copybook—a book students used to practise handwriting

corduroy road—logs laid across wet land and muddy parts of a road

D

driveshaft—a strong bar that was turned by a waterwheel or steam engine; it turned a set of gears and pulleys that made machinery move

E

elders—older people who are respected and asked about important decisions

environment—the land, water, air, and living things in a place

explorer—someone who came to find out about a place he or she knew nothing about

F

factories—businesses that used machinery to produce finished products from raw materials

fall fair—a community event to celebrate the harvest in autumn

fur trader—someone who exchanged goods for furs, and then sold the furs

G

general store—a village business selling many different kinds of products

Great Lakes—a group of five large lakes (Superior, Michigan, Huron, Erie, and Ontario)

grist mill—a business that used water power to grind grain into flour

guardian—a person or spirit who looks after someone

H

hand tools—tools that use only a person's strength to do work; for example, a rake

harness-maker—a tradesperson who made the leather collar and straps worn by horses to pull loads

harvest—to gather the crops produced in fields and gardens

history—the study of how people lived and events that happened in the past

I

immigrants—people who come to a new country to live

L

labourers—people who do physical work for someone else

lacrosse—a team game first played by Aboriginal people

legacy—something of value passed down by people who lived before

livestock—the animals on a farm

longhouse—a large home shared by a number of Iroquoian families

lots—measured pieces of land that were given or sold to settlers for building new homes and farms

Loyalists—people who moved to other British colonies when the American colonies separated from Britain

lumber—pieces of cut wood

M

manure—animal waste, used on fields to help plants grow better

merchants—store owners who bought and sold products

mill— a business that used machinery to make a product from a material

millstones—two large stone wheels that ground grain into flour in a grist mill

Mississauga—a group of Anishinabe people in the southern part of Upper Canada who signed treaties to give up land to settlers

N

nutrients—parts of soil that make plants grow healthy and strong

O

oxen—large, strong male cattle used for heavy work

P

planks—strong, thick boards used for building

population—all of the people living in a place

preserve—to keep something from spoiling; some ways to preserve food are drying, freezing, salting, and smoking

R

rapids—places in a river where water flows quickly over rocks

reserves—land set aside for Aboriginal groups as a place to live, hunt, and farm

root cellar—a cool place below ground used for storing vegetables

S

St. Lawrence River—a large river that flows from Lake Ontario to the Atlantic Ocean

sawmill—a business that used water power to saw logs into lumber (boards and planks)

settlers—people who came to a new place to build homes and communities

shanties—small, roughly built shelters

shear—to cut off a sheep's wool

Six Nations—six Iroquoian-speaking Aboriginal groups that lived south of Lake Ontario before 1783

spinning—twisting fibres tightly together to make a strong yarn or thread

spirits—forces that could not be seen, for which Aboriginal people had special respect

stagecoach—a covered, horse-drawn vehicle that carried people and mail

steam engines—machines that used the pressure from hot steam to move a driveshaft

symbol—a picture or sign that stands for something

T

tallow—cooked animal fat used to make candles, lamp oil, and other products

tanning—a process for making animal skins into leather

team—two or more animals or people working together

threshing—separating grain kernels from their outer coverings and straw

townships—large pieces of land that were measured and divided into lots for settlers

tradespeople—people with special skills and their own tools

trading—exchanging goods you have for other goods that you need

treaties—agreements to give up land in exchange for something

turbine—a type of waterwheel made of iron rather than wood

typhus—a serious disease passed from person to person by body lice

U

Upper Canada—the name used for the part of Ontario near the St. Lawrence River

utensils—tools used in the kitchen

V

vision quest—a young Aboriginal man's journey in search of a picture message from a spirit

W

waterwheel—a large wooden wheel turned by the force of moving water that provided power for a mill

well sweep—a long pole on a Y-shaped support that was used to get water from a well

Wendat—a group of Iroquoian-speaking Aboriginal people (also called Huron)

wigwam—an Anishinabe home built in the shape of a dome or a cone

work bee—neighbours working together to do a large job

Index

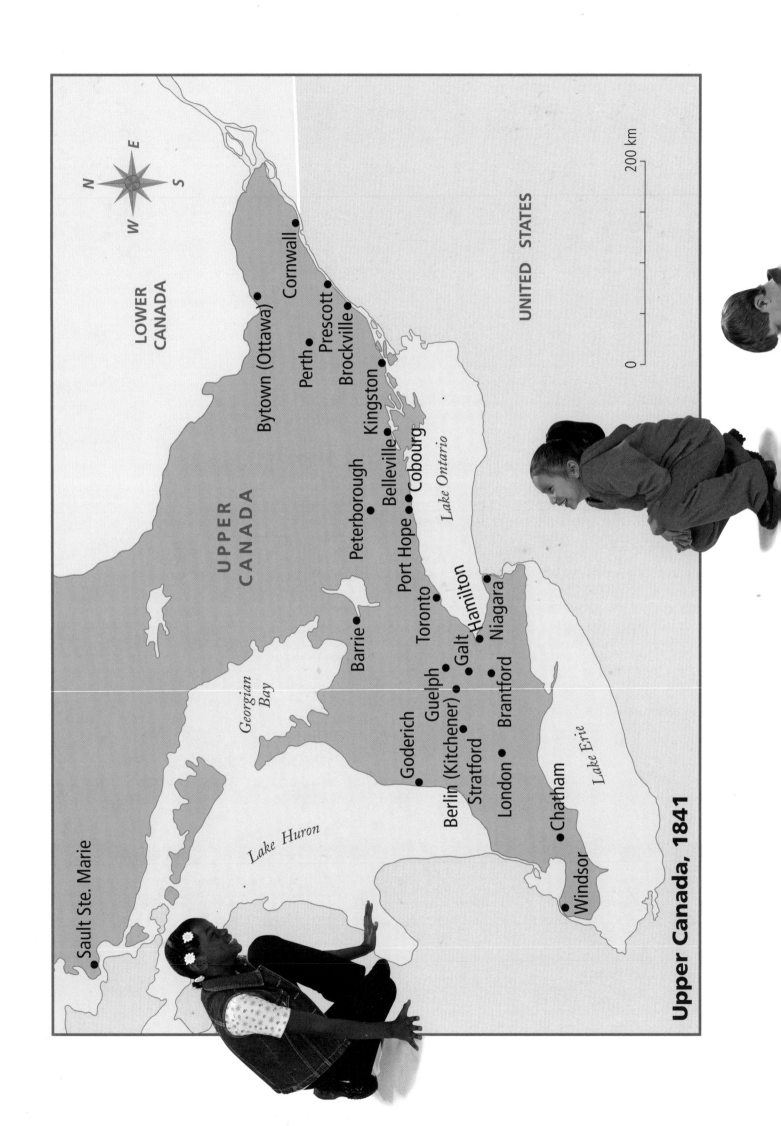

Upper Canada, 1841

Sault Ste. Marie

Lake Huron

Georgian Bay

LOWER CANADA

UPPER CANADA

Bytown (Ottawa)

Cornwall

Perth

Prescott

Brockville

Kingston

Peterborough

Belleville

Port Hope

Cobourg

Lake Ontario

Barrie

Toronto

Hamilton

Galt

Niagara

Guelph

Berlin (Kitchener)

Goderich

Stratford

Brantford

London

Chatham

Windsor

Lake Erie

UNITED STATES

200 km

0